CU00594902

NUTSHELLS

EVIDENCE

IN A

NUTSHELL

AUSTRALIA
The Law Book Company
Brisbane ● Sydney ● Melbourne ● Perth

CANADA AND USA
Carswell
Toronto

NEW ZEALAND
Brooker's
Auckland

SINGAPORE AND MALAYSIA
Thompson Information (S.E. Asia)
Singapore

NUTSHELLS

EVIDENCE
IN A NUTSHELL

SECOND EDITION

by

Christina McAlhone

and

Dr Michael Stockdale,
Senior Lecturers in Law,
University of Northumbria
at Newcastle

London ● Sweet & Maxwell ● 1999

Published in 1999 by
Sweet & Maxwell Limited of
100 Avenue Road, London NW3 3PF
Phototypeset by
Wyvern 21 Limited, Bristol
Printed in England by Clays Ltd, St Ives plc

A CIP Catalogue record
for this book is available
from the British Library

ISBN 0–421–649909

CONTENTS

1. BURDEN AND STANDARD OF PROOF

In legal proceedings, whether civil or criminal, it is necessary to determine which party has the burden of proving the facts in issue and what standard of proof is required.

CIVIL PROCEEDINGS

Burden of proof

In civil proceedings, the position is essentially that the party who raises an issue bears the burden of proving the facts in issue (see *Wakelin v. London and South Western Railway* (1886). Thus, for example, if the plaintiff asserts that he and the defendant formed a contract and that he suffered loss in consequence of the defendant's breach, it is for the plaintiff to prove that the contract was formed, that it was breached by the defendant and that he did suffer loss in consequence of that breach.

What is the effect of the defendant denying the plaintiff's assertions? If the defendant merely denies the plaintiff's assertions, this does not impose a burden of proof upon the plaintiff. Thus, for example, if the defendant claims that no contract was ever formed between himself and the plaintiff it is still the plaintiff who is required to prove the existence of the contract and not the defendant who is required to establish its non-existence. The plaintiff may fail to satisfy the burden proof imposed upon him even if the defendant adduces no evidence and even though defence counsel does not cross-examine the plaintiff's witnesses. As a matter of sensible tactics, however, the defendant will normally do all that he can to rebut the plaintiff's case, where appropriate both cross-examining the plaintiff's witnesses and calling his own.

What is the position where the defendant raises an issue? Where the defendant puts forward a defence which goes beyond a mere denial of the plaintiff's case and actually raises new issues which the plaintiff did not raise, then the defendant does bear the burden of proving the relevant facts in issue. For example, if the defendant claims that the contract which he made with the plaintiff was frustrated, it is for him to prove that a frustrating event made its performance illegal or impossible. In such circumstances the defendant's assertion does not impose a burden of proof on the plaintiff, though, again, as a matter of sensible tactics, the plaintiff will normally do all that he can to negate the defendant's defence.

Does the concept of burden of proof become more important where there is little or no evidence in relation to an issue?

Where there is little or no evidence in relation to an issue, the court may be unable to determine which version of the facts is correct. In such circumstances, the party who bears the burden of proof in relation to the relevant issue must have failed to satisfy it.

At times it may be unclear where the burden of proof lies with regard to an issue in relation to which little or no evidence is available. In such circumstances, when the court determines where the burden of proof lies it may also effectively be deciding the case before it. For example, in *Joseph Constantine Steamship Line Ltd v. Imperial Smelting Corporation Ltd* (1942), the House of Lords was required to consider whether, where a defendant had raised the defence of frustration, he was merely required to prove that a frustrating event had taken place or whether the defence failed unless the defendant also proved that the frustrating event was not his fault. The case concerned the loss of a ship and there was little evidence before the court in relation to the issue of fault. If the burden of proving absence of fault fell on the defendant, then it would be difficult or impossible for defendants to maintain the defence in such circumstances. Conversely, if the burden of proving fault in order to negate the defence of frustration fell on the plaintiff, then, in such circumstances, the defence of frustration would, potentially, be available to defendants. The House of Lords, for a variety of reasons, held that the burden of proving fault lay on the plaintiff.

Finally, it should be noted that where a party to civil proceedings bears the burden of proving facts in issue (sometimes known as the legal burden of proof) it is for the judge to determine whether the party has proved the relevant issue to the standard required by law. Normally, the judge will decide whether the party has satisfied the burden of proof following consideration of all of the relevant evidence (both that adduced by the plaintiff and that adduced by the defendant).

Exceptionally, however, following completion of the plaintiff's case, the defendant may submit that there is no case for him to answer. If the case is being tried by a jury and the plaintiff has not adduced sufficient evidence to raise a prima facie case on his behalf the judge will withdraw the case from the jury (*Alexander v. Rayson* (1936)). The plaintiff may be said to have failed to satisfy the "evidential burden" (*i.e.* the burden of adducing sufficient evidence to entitle the jury to make a finding on his behalf).

Normally, however, there will be no jury. Rather, the judge will be the tribunal of fact. In these circumstances, the judge should not rule on the submission of no case to answer unless the defence call no evidence (*Alexander v. Rayson*).

Standard of proof

The standard of proof in civil proceedings is proof on a balance of probabilities. Thus, the evidence adduced by the party who bears the burden of proof must persuade the judge that it is more probable than not that the facts were as that party asserts (see *Miller v. Minister of Pensions* (1947)). Consequently, where the evidence before the court equally supports the version of the facts put forward by the party who bears the burden of proof and the version put forward by the other party, the party who bears the burden of proof has failed to satisfy it (see *Wakelin v. London and South Western Railway* (1886)). Equally, even though the evidence adduced by the party who bears the burden of proof is more persuasive than that adduced in rebuttal by the other party, the party who bears the burden of proof still fails to satisfy it if the evidence which he adduces does not persuade the judge that his version of the facts is more probably true than not (see *Rhesa Shipping Co SA v. Edmunds* (1985)).

Exceptionally, the standard of proof required in civil proceedings may be the criminal standard of proof, namely, proof beyond reasonable doubt. This may be the case either where this higher standard of proof is required in civil proceedings by statute or where the common law exceptionally so requires. Thus, for example, the criminal standard of proof is required in order to prove contempt of court in civil proceedings (*Re Bramblevale Ltd* (1970)).

Finally, it appears that where criminal conduct is alleged in civil proceedings the requisite standard of proof remains the civil standard, not the criminal standard (see *Hornal v. Neuberger Products Ltd* (1957)). Even so, it should be noted that that, in practice, the more serious the allegation with which a civil court is faced, the more difficult it will be for the party who bears the burden of proving the truth of that allegation to persuade the court of the probability of its truth (see *Hornal v. Neuberger Products Ltd*).

CRIMINAL PROCEEDINGS

Burden of proof

In criminal proceedings, the position is essentially that, subject to limited exceptions, the burden of proof lies on the prosecution (*Woolmington v. DPP* (1935)). Thus, for example, if the accused is charged with murder, it is for the prosecution to prove that the accused unlawfully killed the victim with malice aforethought.

What is the effect of the accused denying part or all of the prosecution's case? If the accused merely denies part or all of the prosecution's case, this does not impose a burden of proof upon the accused. Thus, for example, if the accused claims that he did not kill the victim, it is still the prosecution who is required to prove that the accused did kill the victim and not the accused who is required to prove that he did not. The prosecution may fail to satisfy the burden of proof imposed upon it even if the accused adduces no evidence and even though his counsel does not cross-examine prosecution witnesses. As a matter of sensible tactics, however, the accused will normally do all that he can to rebut the prosecution's case, where appropriate both cross-examining prosecution witnesses and calling his own.

What is the position where the accused raises an issue? Where the accused puts forward a defence which goes beyond a mere denial of the prosecution's case and actually raises new issues which the prosecution did not raise, then, even so, the accused will not normally bear the burden of proving the relevant facts in issue. Rather, provided that there is some evidence before the court upon which a properly directed jury would be entitled to find that the accused's defence was established, the normal rule is that the burden of rebutting the defence lies on the prosecution.

In other words, in such circumstances, the accused may be said to bear the "evidential burden" of adducing sufficient evidence to raise the defence, but if sufficient evidence to raise the defence is before the court then the prosecution bears the "legal burden" of disproving it. In reality, however, even if the defence fails to raise such a defence, the trial judge should still leave the defence to the jury if it is raised by the evidence before the court (*Bullard v. R.* (1957)). Thus, for example, where, upon a charge of murder, the accused claims that he was provoked, it is for the prosecution to prove that the accused was not provoked, not for the accused to prove that he was; provided that the prosecution is not required to disprove provocation unless the evidence before the court raises the defence (*R. v. Mancini* (1942)).

In what circumstances does the accused bear the burden of proving facts in issue? The accused bears the burden of establishing the defence of insanity (*McNaghten's Case* (1843)). Otherwise, the accused only bears the burden of proving facts in issue if this is imposed upon him by statute. For example, section 2(2) of the Homicide Act 1957 expressly places the burden of proving diminished responsibility on the accused.

Where a statute does not expressly place the burden of proving facts in issue upon the accused, it may do so by implication, though a judge should not readily infer that a statutory provision is of this effect (*R. v. Hunt* (1987)). Essentially, it appears that where statute prohibits conduct of a certain type other than in specified exceptional circumstances, it will be for the accused to prove that he falls within the relevant exception (*R. v. Edwards* (1975)). Whether a statutory provision does have this effect, however, fundamentally depends upon the construction of its specific provisions (*R. v. Hunt*).

Thus, for example, where an accused is charged with selling liquor without a licence, the prosecution, in order to succeed, are merely required to prove that the accused sold liquor and are not required to prove that, at the time of the sale, the accused did not possess a licence (*R. v. Edwards*). Rather, if the accused wishes to rely upon the possession of a licence in answer to the case against him, it is for him to prove that he did possess one at the relevant time.

[**Note:** section 101 of the Magistrates' Court Act 1980 provides, essentially, that where an accused relies upon such an exception in summary proceedings, the burden of proving the exception lies upon him. This provision effectively equates with the common law position encountered in relation to trial on indictment (*R. v. Hunt*).]

Does the concept of burden of proof become more important where there is little or no evidence in relation to an issue? Where there is little or no evidence in relation to an issue, the court may be unable to determine which version of the facts is correct. In such circumstances, the party who bears the burden of proof in relation to the relevant issue must have failed to satisfy it.

In *R. v. Edwards* (considered above), neither party had adduced evidence to prove that the accused did or did not possess a licence to sell intoxicating liquor. Thus, if the burden of proving that the accused did not possess such a licence had fallen on th prosecution, then the prosecution would have failed to prove an essential ingredient of its case. As was noted above, however, the Court of Appeal held that it was for the accused to prove that he did possess a licence if he wished to rely upon such possession in answer to the case against him.

Where a party to criminal proceedings bears the burden of proving facts in issue it is for the jury to determine whether the party has proved the relevant issue to the standard required by law. Normally, the jury will decide whether the party has satisfied the burden of proof following consideration of all of the relevant evidence (both that adduced by the prosecution and that adduced by the defence). At times, however, following completion of the prosecution's case, the accused may submit that there is no case for him to answer. In such circumstances, if the prosecution has not adduced sufficient evidence to raise a prima facie case then the judge will withdraw the case or, as appropriate, the relevant count, from the jury (*R. v. Galbraith* (1981)). The prosecution may be said to have failed to satisfy the "evidential burden" (*i.e.* the burden of adducing sufficient evidence to entitle a properly directed jury to make a finding on the prosecution's behalf).

Standard of proof

Where the burden of proof lies on the prosecution, the standard of proof in criminal proceedings is proof beyond reasonable doubt. The other words, if there is more than a remote possibility of the accused's innocence, then he should be found not guilty (*Miller v. Minister of Pensions*). Another way of expressing this standard of proof is to state that the jury must be "satisfied so that they feel sure" of the accused's guilt (*R. v. Summers* (1952)).

Where the burden of proof lies on the accused, the standard of proof in criminal proceedings is proof on a balance of probabilities (*R. v. Carr-Briant* (1943)).

---

2. COMPETENCE AND COMPELLABILITY

Most persons are both competent to give evidence in civil or criminal proceedings and can be compelled to do so. In this chapter we will consider those exceptional classes of person who either are not competent witnesses (*i.e.* persons who cannot give evidence) or who, whilst competent witnesses, are not compellable (*i.e.* persons who may choose to give evidence but cannot be required to do so).

THE ACCUSED

Can the accused testify for the prosecution?

Neither the accused (*R. v. Rhodes* (1899)) nor any person jointly charged with him in criminal proceedings (*R. v. Sharrock* (1948)) is a competent prosecution witness. Thus, if A and B are jointly tried, neither A nor B may give evidence for the prosecution. B may be compelled to give evidence for the prosecution against A, however, if B pleads guilty, if B has already been acquitted of the relevant charge or charges or if the proceedings against B have been discontinued. Moreover, B may be compelled to give evidence for the prosecution against A if A and B are being tried separately.

[***Note***: if B pleads guilty but is not to be sentenced until after he has given evidence for the prosecution against A or if A and B are being tried separately and B is not to be tried until after he has given evidence for the prosecution against A, then B may be tempted to distort the evidence he gives against A in his own favour. It was at one time thought that in such circumstances the trial judge should in the former situation sentence B prior to permitting him to testify and in the latter not permit B to testify unless the prosecution agreed to drop the proceedings against him (*R. v. Pipe* (1966)). Modern judicial practice appears to be, however, that, in the former situation, the trial judge is entitled to sentence B either before he testifies or at the end of the trial after hearing all of the evidence and that in the latter situation the judge is entitled to receive B's evidence in the absence of such an undertaking (*Chan Wai-keung v. R.* (1995); *R. v. Turner* (1975)).]

Can the accused be a defence witness?

The accused is a competent defence witness but cannot be compelled to give evidence (section 1, Criminal Evidence Act 1898). Thus, if A and B are jointly tried, B may choose to give evidence for the defence but cannot be compelled to do so by A. If an accused does not testify in his own defence, however, the court may be entitled to draw an inference from his silence (see Chapter 3 below).

THE SPOUSE OF THE ACCUSED

The position of the accused's spouse (husband or wife) in criminal
proceedings is governed by section 80 of the Police and Criminal
Evidence Act 1984.

Can the accused's spouse testify for the prosecution?

Section 80 makes the accused's spouse competent to give evidence
for the prosecution unless the two spouses are jointly charged with
an offence. Even if the accused's spouse is competent to give evidence for the prosecution, the spouse can only be compelled to give
evidence for the prosecution if the offence charged is of a type
specified by section 80(3) (for example, if it involved an assault on
the spouse or on a person under the age of 16 or if it is a sexual
offence alleged to have been committed in respect of a person
under the age of 16).

[*Note*: whether the spouse is a competent prosecution witness
when the accused and the spouse are charged with different
offences in the same indictment is unclear. Similarly, it is not clear
whether the spouse is a competent and compellable prosecution
witness when the accused and the spouse are charged with different
offences in the same indictment and section 80(3) is applicable.]

Can the accused's spouse be a defence witness?

Section 80 makes the accused's spouse competent to give evidence
for the defence (both for the accused and for any persons jointly
charged with the accused). The accused's spouse may be compelled
to give evidence for the accused unless the two spouses are jointly
charged with an offence. The accused's spouse may be compelled
to give evidence for a person jointly charged with the accused only
if the offence charged is of a type specified by section 80(3) (see
above). Where, however, the accused and another are charged in
the same indictment with different offences, it has been held by
the Court of Appeal that section 80(3) does not apply and that,
consequently, the accused's spouse is compellable to give evidence
for the co-accused even though the relevant offence does not fall
within section 80(3) (*R. v. Woolgar* (1991)).

[*Note*: whether the spouse can be compelled to give evidence for
the accused when the accused and the spouse are charged with

different offences in the same indictment is unclear. Similarly, it is not clear whether the spouse can be compelled to give evidence for a person jointly charged with the accused when the accused and the spouse are charged with different offences in the same indictment and section 80(3) is applicable.]

Former spouses and spouses who refuse to testify

Section 80(5) provides that a former spouse of the accused is competent and compellable as if the accused and the former spouse had never been married. Finally, section 80(8) provides that the prosecution cannot comment upon the failure of the accused's spouse to testify.

LIMITED MENTAL ABILITY AND COMMUNICATION DIFFICULTIES

A person called to give evidence in legal proceedings who, in the opinion of the judge, does not sufficiently appreciate the seriousness of the occasion or does not realise that giving evidence under oath involves more than the everyday duty of telling the truth is not competent (see *R. v. Bellamy* (1986)). In determining the competence of a witness, the judge may examine the witness and hear expert psychological evidence in the absence of the jury (*R. v. Deakin* (1994); *R. v. Hampshire* (1995)). Indeed, if the witness is mentally ill, it may be that the judge, having heard the evidence of the expert, can deal with the issue of competence without the necessity of examining the witness (*R. v. Barratt* (1996)). If the witness's incapacity is only short term, *e.g.* when it is caused by drink or drugs, the judge may be prepared to adjourn (*R. v. Baines* (1987)).

A person incapable of communicating his evidence to the court, *e.g.* because the person is deaf and dumb and is incapable of communicating by sign language through an interpreter, is also incompetent (*R. v. Whitehead* (1866)).

CHILDREN

Children in criminal proceedings

Section 33A of the Criminal Justice Act 1988 (as amended by the Criminal Justice and Public Order Act 1994) provides that, in criminal proceedings, a child (that is, a person under fourteen years of age) may not give sworn evidence but may give unsworn evidence unless in the opinion of the judge the child is incapable of giving intelligible testimony. Essentially, it appears that the judge must consider whether the child can understand questions put to him and can answer them coherently and comprehensibly (*DPP v. M.* (1996)). The judge may decide to examine the child before he testifies, the presence of the jury not being essential, or may decide to permit the child to testify without undertaking such an examination, subject to the possibility of standing the child down and striking his testimony out if it proves to be unintelligible (*R. v. Hampshire* (1995)).

Children in civil proceedings

The position in civil proceedings is a little more complicated than that encountered in the criminal context. First, a child (a person under the age of 18—Children Act 1989, s.105) may be competent to give sworn testimony. This will be the case if, in the opinion of the judge, the child sufficiently appreciates the seriousness of the occasion and realises that giving evidence under oath involves more than the everyday duty of telling the truth (see *R. v. Hayes* (1977) and *R. v. Campbell* (1983)). Secondly, if a child is not competent to give sworn testimony, the child may give unsworn testimony if, in the opinion of the judge, the child both understands that he is under a duty to speak the truth and has sufficient understanding to justify the reception of his evidence (Children Act 1989, s.96). Finally, if a child is neither competent to give sworn testimony nor competent to give unsworn testimony then the child is incompetent and its evidence may not be received.

---

3. CORROBORATION AND SUPPORTING EVIDENCE, IDENTIFICATION EVIDENCE, THE ACCUSED'S RIGHTS OF SILENCE AND HIS LIES

CORROBORATION

What is corroborative evidence?

Essentially, one item of evidence is corroborated by another when the reliability of the former is confirmed by the latter. In English

Law, however, in order for one piece of admissible evidence to be capable of corroborating another, the corroborating evidence must, as was recognised by the Court of Criminal Appeal in *R. v. Baskerville* (1916), satisfy two fundamental requirements.

(1) The corroborative evidence must be independent of the witness whose evidence requires corroboration.

(2) The corroborative evidence must connect the accused with the commission of the crime by confirming in a material particular both that the crime was committed and that it was committed by the accused.

Corroborative evidence is now rarely required

In English Law, corroborative evidence is only required in those exceptional situations in which statute has imposed a corroboration requirement. For example, a person cannot be convicted of speeding if the only evidence that he was speeding is the uncorroborated evidence of a single witness (Road Traffic Regulation Act 1984, s.89). Thus, D cannot be convicted of speeding solely upon the evidence of W, who is prepared to testify that he saw D exceeding the speed limit, but D may be convicted if W's evidence is confirmed by X, who was with W when D's car passed them, or if W's evidence is confirmed by some mechanical means (*e.g.* by the speedometer of W's car or by a speed gun) (see *Nicholas v. Penny* (1950)).

Corroboration warnings are no longer required

The common law does not require the corroboration of a witness's evidence though, until recently, a trial judge was required to warn the jury of the danger of convicting upon the uncorroborated evidence of three classes of witness. The relevant classes of witness were chidlren, accomplices of the accused who were giving evidence for the prosecution and sexual offence complainants. The judge was required to explain to the jury why it was dangerous to convict upon the uncorroborated evidence of the relevant witness, to explain what was meant by corroboration and to identify for the jury evidence capable in law of providing corroboration. It was for the jury to decide whether the potentially corroborative evidence identified by the judge did, in fact, corroborate the evidence of the relevant witness. Moreover, even if the jury rejected the potentially corroborative evidence or if there was no evidence capable in law of providing corroboration, the jury were still entitled to convict solely upon the evidence of the relevant witness if they accepted it. Further, the courts also recognised that where an unreliable witness did not fall within one of these three classes it might still be necessary for the trial judge to give the jury an appropriate warning (for example: in consequence of the mental state of the witness (*R. v. Spencer*; *R. v. Smails* (1987)); where the witness is a co-accused giving evidence against the accused (*R. v. Cheema* (1994)); or, if the witness may have an improper purpose of his own to serve when giving evidence against the accused (*R. v. Beck* (1982)))).

When should a judge warn the jury of the dangers of relying on a witness's evidence and what form should the warning take?

Statutory reform has recently abolished the requirement that the judge give the jury a corroboration warning in respect of the evidence of witnesses falling within one or more of these three categories, rendering the concept of corroboration in its technical legal sense of extremely limited significance in criminal proceedings.

First, section 34(2) of the Criminal Justice Act 1988 (as amended by the Criminal Justice and Public Order Act 1994) removed the requirement that the judge give a warning in respect of convicting upon the uncorroborated evidence of a child. Once this provision came into force, the only remaining classes of witness in respect of whose evidence a corroboration warning was required were the accomplice who gave evidence for the prosecution and the sexual offence complainant (see *R. v. Pryce* (1991). Secondly, section 32(1) of the Criminal Justice and Public Order Act 1994 removed the requirements that the judge give a warning in respect of convicting upon the uncorroborated evidence of an accomplice who gave evidence for the prosecution or that of a sexual offence complainant.

The extent to which a trial judge should now give some form of warning following the abolition of these final two warning requirements was recently considered by the Court of Appeal in *R. v. Makanjuola* (1995). So far as the need to warn the jury is concerned, their Lordships made clear that whilst the judge possesses discretion to give a warning, he will not be required to do so simply because the witness is an accomplice of the accused who is testifying for the prosecution or is a sexual offence complainant. Rather, a warning is appropriate where there is an evidential basis for suggesting that a witness's evidence is unreliable. This may, for example, be revealed by the content and quality of the witness's evidence or by evidence revealing that he has a grudge against the accused or that she has made false sexual offence complaints in the past. Presumably, evidence of the witness's mental state or evidence suggesting that the witness may have an improper purpose of his own to serve in giving evidence against the accused will, potentially, remain equally relevant in this context.

So far as the nature of the warning is concerned, their Lordships made clear that a formal corroboration is no longer required. Thus, it is no longer necessary either to explain what is meant by evidence capable of providing corroboration. Rather, when a trial judge in the exercise of his discretion decides that a warning is required, the warning should form part of his review of and comments upon the evidence and the nature of the warning is for the judge to determine. Thus, it might be sufficient simply to urge the jury to be cautious when considering placing reliance upon the evidence of the relevant witness. Alternatively, the judge may feel that it is necessary to advise the jury to look for evidence supporting that of the relevant witness before placing reliance upon it. It appears, however, that evidence which is not independent is not capable of amounting to supporting evidence (*R. v. Islam* (1998)). Thus, if C tells W that she was indecently assaulted by D and C then testifies to this effect, W's repetition of C's statement to him in court is not independent evidence and thus is not capable of amounting to evidence of the facts complained of, though it may be admissible as evidence of C's consistency (see Chapter 4 below).

IDENTIFICATION EVIDENCE

What are the "Turnbull guidelines?"

The Court of Appeal in *R. v. Turnbull* (1977) laid down guidelines which are applicable when the prosecution's case against the accused is wholly or substantially based upon disputed identification evidence. Essentially, the trial judge should warn the jury to be cautious when considering placing reliance upon the evidence of one or more witnesses who have identified the accused, explaining to them that such witnesses may be both convincing and mistaken. The judge should direct the jury to consider the circumstances in which an observation was made. Thus, they should be directed to consider factors such as: the duration of the period of observation; the distance between the witness and the person observed; the quality of the light; whether the observation was impeded in any way; whether the witness knew the accused and, if so, how many times they had met or how memorable their meetings had been;

the length of time between the observation and the witness identifying the accused to the police; and any material discrepancies between the witness's description to the police of the person observed and the actual appearance of the accused. Further, where the witness did know the accused at the time when the observation was made, the jury should be reminded that people do sometimes make mistakes in recognising friends and relatives.

Where identification evidence is of good quality (*e.g.* when the observation was made in good lighting by a friend of the accused who had a clear view of him a short distance away for several minutes) it is safe to leave the evidence to the jury provided that they have been given a warning in the terms outlined by the Court of Appeal (though no particular form of words is required). Where the quality of the identification evidence is poor, however, (*e.g.* where the witness only had a fleeting glance of the person he observed or where the observation was made at a long distance and in bad light by a stranger), simply to warn the jury in the terms outlined by the Court of Appeal is not sufficient. Rather, in such circumstances, the judge should withdraw the case from the jury and direct them to acquit the accused unless there is other evidence which is capable of supporting the identification evidence. Where such evidence exists the judge should direct the jury's attention to it but the judge should also direct them to ignore for this purpose any evidence which they might regard as providing support for an identification which does not in fact do so. Examples of potentially supporting evidence are the evidence of other identification witnesses (though the jury should be warned that they all may be mistaken—see *R. v. Weeder* (1980) and *R. v. Breslin* (1984)) and, in certain circumstances, lies told by the accused (see below)).

Do the "Turnbull guidelines" apply to forms of identification other than identification of the accused by witnesses?

Where a witness identifies the accused from a photograph or video recording, the Turnbull guidelines are applicable (see, respectively, *R. v. Blenkinsop* (1995) and *Taylor v. Chief Constable of Cheshire* (1987)). Similarly, an appropriately modified version of the Turnbull guidelines is applicable in the context of voice identification by witnesses (*R. v. Hersey* (1998)). Where, however, the jury themselves make an identification from a photograph or video recording without the assistance of a witness, it appears that the Turnbull guidelines are not applicable (see *R. v. Downey* (1995)). In such circumstances, however, the judge should, even so, direct the jury to consider factors such as the quality of the image and any change in the appearance of the accused between the time when the photograph or video recording was taken and the time of the trial (see *R. v. Dodson* (1984)).

Moreover, if there is strong evidence to the effect that the accused and another person were together at the time when the offence with which the accused is charged was committed and evidence identifying the other person is disputed, it appears that a Turnbull warning is required if the accused claims that he was not present (*R. v. Bath* (1990)).

Finally, it should be noted that where a witness identified not the accused but a car, whilst the Turnbull guidelines are not applicable, the jury should be directed to consider factors such as the opportunity which the witness had to identify the vehicle and the ability of the witness to distinguish between cars (*R. v. Browning* (1991)).

THE ACCUSED'S RIGHT OF SILENCE

Until very recently it was a basic tenet of English common law that a person could remain silent when faced with an allegation of criminal conduct and, should he be prosecuted for that offence, no adverse inferences could be drawn from his silence except in very exceptional circumstances (see *Hall v. R.* (1971)). The Criminal Justice and Public Order Act 1994 (CJPOA) altered the common law position, however, so as to permit the drawing of adverse inferences and has differentiated between silence outside the court and at the trial itself. Thus, it is necessary to consider the relevance of the accused's silence both inside and outside the courtroom.

Silence outside the court

This involves a consideration of the effect of the accused's silence both in respect to an allegation made by an ordinary member of the public and in response to an allegation made by a police officer or other person charged with the duty of investigating offences.

Silence in response to an allegation not made by a person in authority

What does the CJPOA say? Section 34(5) covers the position in which the accused remains silent prior to caution and, therefore, effectively encompasses allegations put by someone other than a policeman (who would have to caution a suspect before putting an allegation to him).

Section 34(5) basically states that the common law regarding any adverse inferences which could be drawn in this situation is unaffected by the statute. Thus, it is necessary to consider the common law rules which the statute preserves.

What is the common law position? In *Hall v. R.*, the Privy Council was prepared to recognise that in very exceptional circumstances an adverse inference could be drawn from silence but did not elaborate on what this might entail. However, the Privy Council did provide an explanation in *Parkes v. R.* (1976). The case involved a confrontation in the street between the accused and the victim's mother. The court held that adverse inferences could be drawn from the accused's silence in response to the mother's allegation that he had killed her daughter, the reason being that the parties had been "speaking on even terms".

This "even terms" principle, as it has become known, means that if an accusation of criminal conduct is put by someone who is not in authority or not charged with investigating crimes and the accused makes no reply, the court can draw adverse inferences from his silence on the basis that an innocent man would surely utter some denial in such circumstances.

Silence as to a fact later relied upon by the accused in his defence

Section 34(1) & (2) allows the court, in assessing guilt, to "draw such inferences ... as appear proper" from evidence that the accused, when questioned under caution either:

    (a) prior to being charged, failed to mention any fact subsequently relied on in his defence in those proceedings OR

    (b) on being charged with the offence or officially informed that he might be prosecuted for it, failed the mention any such fact.

In either case (a) or (b) above, the fact must be one which was known to the accused at the time he is questioned under caution and which, in the circumstances existing at the time, the accused could reasonably have been expected to mention.

[*Note:* silence as to a relevant fact cannot, on its own, form the basis of a conviction or constitute a prima facie case against the accused (see section 38(3)), and the trial judge retains the power to prevent the drawing of inferences in the exercise of his discretion, see section 38(6).]

In *R. v. Argent* (1997), the Court of Appeal held that the term 'circumstances existing at the time' should not be construed too narrowly and could, where relevant, include the time of day and the defendant's age, experience, state of health, mental capacity, sobriety, tiredness, knowledge, personality and access to legal advice.

Remaining silent on solicitor's advice

In *R. v. Condron* (1997), the court held that remaining silent in such circumstances was unlikely, on its own, to be regarded as sufficient grounds for not mentioning a relevant fact. It would be necessary to go further and adduce evidence as to the reason for the advice and, in doing so, waive legal professional privilege. However, even where the advice of the solicitor is considered reasonable by the court, this will not be decisive as what is paramount is the reasonableness of the accused's conduct in the circumstances (see *R. v. Argent*).

The trial judge's direction to the jury under section 34

The court held in *R. v. Condron* (1997) that the trial judge should direct the jury that it is for them to decide whether to draw an inference adverse to the accused under section 34 but that they should only do so where they include that there is no other sensible explanation for the accused's silence other than his guilt or that he has subsequently fabricated the account relied upon. In *R. v. Daniel* (1998) it was held that the jury may also draw an inference where they conclude that there has been earlier fabrication of facts relied on by the defence but that the accused did not mention such facts at interview in the belief, for example, that they would not stand up to further questioning.

Silence in response to a request to account for objects, substances, marks or one's presence at a particular place

An inference may be drawn from the accused's failure or refusal to account for objects, substances or marks under section 36 provided that the following conditions are satisfied:

(i) The accused must have been under arrest.
(ii) An object, substance or mark must have been found at the place of the accused's arrest either in his possession, on his person, clothing or footwear.
(iii) The constable or Customs and Excise officer investigating the offence must have reasonably believed that the presence of the object etc. might be due to the participation of the accused in the commission of an offence he has specified and have so informed him.
(iv) Following a warning in plain language of the effect of his failure to do so, the constable or Customs and Excise officer must have asked the accused to account for the presence of the object, etc., and he failed or refused to so account.

An inference may be drawn from the accused's failure to account for his presence at the scene of the crime under section 37 provided that the following conditions are satisfied:

(i) the accused must have been under arrest.
(ii) He must have been found at a place, at or about, the time the offence was alleged to have occurred.
(iii) The constable or Customs and Excise officer investigating the offence must reasonably have believed that the accused's presence at the scene was due to his participation in the offence and have so informed him.
(iv) Following a warning in plain language of the effect of his failure to do so, the constable or officer of Customs and Excise must have asked the accused to account for his presence and he failed or refused to so account.

The trial judge's direction to the jury under sections 36 and 37

Although the courts have yet to consider these two sections it is likely that when they do so they will decide that the appropriate direction is one similar to that under section 34, see above.

[**Note:** An inference drawn from the accused's silence under section 36 or section 37 cannot, on its own, constitute a prima facie case against the accused although it can contribute to a prima facie against him, see section 38(3). Further, the trial judge retains the power to prevent the drawing of an inference under either section in the exercise if his discretion (see section 38(6).]

The accused's silence at trial

What does the CJPOA say? The relevant provision is section 35 which permits inferences to be drawn at trial from the accused's failure to testify at all or to answer questions once he has taken the stand. Such silence cannot contribute to a prima facie case or form the sole basis of a conviction, see section 38(3). Adverse inferences may only be drawn if the following conditions are satisfied:

   (i) The accused's guilt is in issue and the accused's physical or mental condition is not such that it appears to the court undesirable for him to give evidence.

(ii) Also, where the accused takes the stand but refuses to answer any questions, he must not have had a good cause for his refusal. This means that an inference may not be drawn from the accused's refusal to answer questions which he is not legally obliged to answer.

In *R. v. Cowan* (1995), the Court of Appeal rejected a defence submission that section 35 has reversed the burden of proof and that it should be confined to exceptional circumstances. The court recognised the trial judge's exclusionary discretion under section 35 but a further defence submission that it should be exercised in favour of an accused with previous convictions was rejected.

THE ACCUSED'S LIES

A jury may be entitled to draw an inference of guilt from lies told by the accused either out of court or in court. It should be noted, however, that the jury should only draw such an inference if they are satisfied beyond reasonable doubt both that the accused did lie and that he lied because he was guilty and not for some other reason (see *R. v. Burge*; *R. v. Pegg* (1995)). Thus, for example, if the jury believe that D, charged with rape, may have lied to the police about having had intercourse with V not because he raped her but because he did not want his wife to find out that he had had intercourse with her, then the jury should not drawn an inference of guilt from D's lie.

A trial judge may, in practice, find it necessary to warn the jury as to the significance of the accused's lies, and, in particular, to warn them that they should only draw an inference of guilt from them if sure both that he lied and that he lied because he was guilty. It appears that the giving of such a warning is usually necessary:

   (i) Where an alibi is raised by the defence;

  (ii) Where the judge advises the jury to look for evidence in support of the evidence of an unreliable witness (including evidence in support of poor quality identification evidence) and identifies lies which the accused has or may have told as potential supporting evidence;

 (iii) Where the prosecution relies upon lies which the accused has or may have told as evidence of his guilt;

 (iv) Where there is a danger that the jury may rely upon lies which the accused may have told as evidence of his guilt (*R. v. Burge*; *R. v. Pegg*).

---

4. EXAMINATION, CROSS-EXAMINATION AND RE-EXAMINATION OF WITNESSES

This Chapter deals with the three stages involved in questioning a witness in both civil and criminal trials:

—*Examination in chief*
—*Cross-examination*
—*Re-examination*

As with many topics in evidence, the issues of admissibility, effect and relevance are of primary importance and must be borne in mind whenever tackling a question on examination of witnesses.

EXAMINATION IN CHIEF

This is the first stage of the process of questioning a witness. Counsel for the party who has called the witness asks him questions in order to elicit from him evidence which is advantageous to that party's case.

The types of questions which may not be asked during examination in chief

The normal rules relating to the admissibility of evidence apply to examination in chief so that the party who has called the witness may not ask him to provide evidence which would be inadmissible at *any* stage of the trial, for example because it is hearsay or similar fact evidence. In addition, there are rules particular to examination in chief which preclude the admission of certain other types of evidence. Thus, leading questions and, subject to exceptions, questions relating to a witness's previous consistent statements are *not* permitted during examination in chief.

Leading questions These are questions which either imply that a certain answer is expected from the witness (*e.g.* "Was the car which knocked you over a blue Rolls Royce?") or which presume certain disputed evidence has been accepted (*e.g.* "Did the defendant drive straight on after he had hit you?")

Such questons are inadmissible because it is not, in effect, the witness giving his own version of the events but rather counsel for the party who called him suggesting what he ought to say. Strictly speaking, preliminary questions about a witness's name and address are leading questions but these are permitted for expediency.

Questions concerning a witness's previous consistent or self serving statements Witnesses may frequently wish to bolster the credibility of their testimony by asserting that what they are now saying is consistent with oral or written statements they have made prior to trial, the hope being that the court is more likely to believe them if they have not wavered in their story. However, questions regarding such previous consistent or "self serving" statements are not permitted during examination in chief, (see *R. v. Roberts* (1942)). The rule also extends to prevent other witnesses testifying regarding the previous consistent statements. In addition to being inadmissible to show consistency, previous consistent statements are also inadmissible to prove the truth of their factual content, being hearsay.

As with many evidential rules, the rule against previous consistent statements has exceptions and these are listed below. Where such an exception applies, a witness may refer in chief to a previous consistent statement in order to show consistency, this being relevant to his credibility. The previous statement will, however, remain hearsay and, consequently, inadmissible as to the truth of its factual content unless an exception to the hearsay rule also applies.

Exceptions
Recent complaints in cases involving sexual offences: Where such recent complaints become admissible, the prosecution may call

the complainant or the person to whom the complaint was made to give evidence of not just the mere fact that the complaint was made but also actual details of the complaint (see *R. v. Lillyman* (1896)). The purpose of adducing evidence of such complaints is, as explained above, to lend credibility to the complainant's testimony. Specifically, where the case involves the issue of consent it will lend credibility to the complainant's allegation of lack of consent, although it will not amount to actual evidence of lack of consent as it would be hearsay if an attempt was made to adduce it for that purpose (see the Australian case of *Kilby v. R.* (1973)).

If this exception is to apply, the following conditions must be met:

(a) The case must involve a sexual offence (*R. v. Osborne* (1905)) although the victim may be of either sex (*R. v. Camelleri* (1922)).

(b) The complainant must testify (*R. v. Wallwork* (1958)).

A previous consistent statement is only relevant to the credibility of the complainant, which is not in issue if he or she does not testify. Thus, the previous statement will be excluded as irrelevant unless the complainant testifies.

(c) The statement must be made voluntarily.

A statement may still be treated as voluntary even if made in answer to a question but only if the question merely anticipates the statement which the witness was about to make in any event (see *R. v. Osborne*).

(d) The statement must be made at the first reasonable opportunity that presents itself.

Where there is some delay between the commission of the offence and the making of the complaint, the court will take into account not only the length of the delay but also the age and state of the complainant, the nature of the offence and the availability of reasonably suitable confidants, in determining whether the complaint was made at the first available opportunity (see *R. v. Cummings* (1948)).

Evidence that the accused has previously been identified: A witness is allowed to state that he has on a previous occasion identified the accused as the offender (see *R. v. Christie* (1914), which involved a street identification).

Statements made in civil proceedings which are adduced with the leave of the court: Section 6(2)(a) of the Civil Evidence Act 1995 provides that a previous consistent statement is admissible in civil proceedings under section 1 of the Act as evidence of the truth of its factual content provided the leave of the court is first obtained. Leave is not required, however, where the statement is used to rebut a suggestion of recent fabrication, see below.

Where it has been suggested in cross-examination that the witness has recently fabricated his testimony. If opposing counsel makes a specific suggestion to a witness that he has recently made up the evidence which he is giving in court, and the witness has in fact already made a statement which is consistent with his present testimony, that previous statement may be admissible to rebut the allegation of recent fabrication (see *R. v. Flanagan v. Fahy* (1918)).

Relevance: The relevance of a previous consistent statement which becomes admissible to rebut a suggestion of recent fabrication depends upon the nature of the proceedings. In criminal proceedings, the previous statement is merely relevant to the credibility of its maker. In civil proceedings, the statement is relevant not only to its maker's credibility but also as to the truth of its factual content without the leave of the court, see section 6(2)(b) of the Civil Evidence Act 1995.

Statements made by an accused during interviews with the police which become admissible at trial will still be admissible even if they contain self-serving statements (see *R. v. Pearce* (1979)).

What can be done if a witness cannot remember what he is supposed to say during examination in chief?

There are two possibilities depending upon whether the witness is experiencing problems remembering before he goes into court or whether he begins to experience difficulties once he has taken the stand.

Refreshing one's memory outside the witness box Before going into court, a witness may read through a documentary statement he has previously made in order to refresh his memory (see *R. v. Richardson* (1971)).

Refreshing one's memory in the witness box Once a witness has begun to testify, he may only refresh his memory from his previous documentary statement with the leave of the court. Before granting leave, the trial judge must be satisfied that the witness prepared the document himself or, if it was prepared by someone else, the witness verified the document whilst the event was still fresh in his memory (see *R. v. Mills* (1962)).

Verification merely involves the witness looking at the document and checking that what it states is correct or having the statement read out to him and then accepting that it is correct (see *R. v. Kelsey* (1982)).

Until very recently the trial judge also had to be satisfied that the memory refreshing document was made contemporaneously with the events it described. However, in *R. v. Da Silva* (1990), the court held that the judge might, in the exercise of his discretion, permit a witness to refresh his memory from a non-contemporaneous statement provided four criteria were satisfied, namely:

(i) the statement was made near the time of the events described;

(ii) the witness is now unable to recall the events in question due to lapse of time;

(iii) the witness did not read through the statement before going into the witness box;

(iv) the witness wishes to read the statement before continuing his or her testimony.

A witness may still be permitted, however, to refresh his or her memory from a non-contemporaneous document even if all four of the above criteria are not met as the matter is entirely one of judicial discretion (see *R. v. South Ribble Magistrate's Court ex parte Cockrane* (1996)).

What can be done if one's witness fails to give the evidence he had been called to give, *i.e.* "fails to come up to proof"?

A witness who fails to come up to proof may either be treated by the court as merely unfavourable or as actually hostile to the party who called him, depending upon the reason for his failure. The distinction between these two types of witness is important as the action which the party who called the witness may take to remedy the situation depends upon how the witness is treated by the court.

Unfavourable witnesses A witness is unfavourable if it is clear to the court either that he does wish to provide favourable evidence but is, for some reason, *e.g.* memory loss, unable to do so or if his testimony is truthful but actually unhelpful to the party who has called him.

Action that may be taken: If a witness proves to be unfavourable there is little that the party who called him can do other than to adduce further evidence to prove that which the witness has failed to prove, for example by calling other witnesses to counteract the evidence of the first (see *Ewer v. Ambrose* (1825) in which a second witness was called to prove the existence of a partnership the first witness having failed to do so).

It is not permitted to discredit one's own witness by attacking his character and credit merely because he is unfavourable. Nor is it permitted to put to him a previous statement he has made which is inconsistent with his present testimony.

Hostile witnesses A witness is described as hostile if he clearly has no wish to tell the truth on behalf of the party who called him.

As a witness will not automatically be treated as hostile, the party who called him must first seek the judge's permission to have the witness declared hostile. The judge will take into account factors such as the witness's degree of co-operation and manner in assessing whether to declare him hostile. If the witness has made a previous inconsistent statement outside court, then, unless the witness is blatantly hostile, the judge and the party calling the witness ought to consider giving the witness the opportunity to refresh his memory from it. If the witness should refuse to do so and also to provide an explanation why his present testimony is inconsistent with his earlier statement, then the judge may consider that he should be declared hostile (see *R. v. Maw* (1994)).

Action that may be taken once a witness has been declared hostile:

(1) Evidence may be adduced to contradict the witness.

(2) With the leave of the judge, the witness may be cross-examined and may be asked leading questions. He cannot, however, be treated in exactly the same way as any witness under cross-examination in that he cannot be discredited by being asked questions about his bad character or previous convictions.

(3) With the leave of the judge, the party who called the witness may prove that the witness has made a previous inconsistent statement. Before doing so, details of the occasion on which the statement was made must be given to the witness so that he may remember making the statement and he must then be asked whether he made such a statement (see section 3 of the Criminal Procedure Act 1865 which applies to both criminal and civil proceedings).

Relevance: The relevance of a previous inconsistent statement made by a hostile witness which becomes admissible in this way depends upon the nature of the proceedings. In criminal proceedings, it is relevant only to the credit of the witness (see *R. v. Golder* (1960)). The judge's role will be to consider whether the witness is at all worthy of belief. If he considers the witness to be sufficiently creditworthy, he should warn the jury of the dangers involved when a witness contradicts himself and direct them to determine whether they can believe such a witness. Only if they consider that they can should they then proceed to assess which aspects of the witness's evidence to accept (see *R. v. Maw*). In civil proceedings, the previous statement is relevant to both credit and to the truth of its factual content (see section 1 of the Civil Evidence Act 1995). The notice requirements provided by section 2 of the Act are unlikely to apply because it is not until the witness actually testifies in court that he or she may be declared hostile. Consequently, notice will not be considered "reasonable and practicable in the circumstances", see further Chapter 9.

What action may be taken if a hostile witness refuses to testify?: Section 3 of the Criminal Procedure Act 1865 is inapplicable in this situation because the witness has not given any testimony with which his previous statement can be inconsistent. Thus, his previous statement may not be adduced under section 3. However, it may be adduced at common law with the leave of the judge. In *R. v. Thompson* (1976), the Court of Appeal held that the judge has a common law discretion to permit cross-examination, including questions about a previous statement, of a hostile witness by the party who has called him.

The video evidence of children: Section 32 of the Criminal Justice Act 1988 permits children and persons overseas to give evidence by live video link in criminal proceedings heard on indictment, by the Court of Appeal or a youth court, if the case involves one of the offences specified by the section (*e.g.* various sexual offences).

Section 32A of the Criminal Justice Act 1988 permits children under 14 (or under 17 if the case involves one of the sexual offences specified by the section) who are to be witnesses in criminal proceedings to be heard on indictment, by the Court of Appeal or a youth court, to be videoed giving their evidence prior to trial. Provided the child is then called as a witness at the trial, the video evidence will stand as his examination in chief. The child can still be cross-examined in the normal way or by a live video link.

CROSS-EXAMINATION

This is the second stage of the process of questioning a witness. It takes place after examination in chief and is the stage where a party may question his opponent's witness in an effort to gain favourable evidence or to undermine the witness's testimony. A party who fails to cross-examine a witness is taken to have accepted the witness's testimony and cannot later dispute it (see *R. v. Bircham* (1972)).

As with examination in chief, the normal rules relating to the admissibility of evidence apply to cross-examination. Unlike examination in chief, however, leading questions are usually allowed during cross-examination.

Witnesses must normally answer any questions which are put to them during cross-examination, even questions aimed at discrediting them.

Two rules relating specifically to cross-examination which are of particular importance for examination purposes are the rule relating to questions concerning collateral matters and the special rule relating to the cross-examination of a complainant in a rape case.

Questions concerning collateral matters

The rule The basic rule with regard to questions concerning collateral matters is that a witness may be asked questions about such matters only during cross-examination but, subject to the exceptions listed below, a witness's answer to such questions will be treated as final so that the cross-examining party may not call evidence in rebuttal (see *R. v. Edwards* (1991)).

What is a collateral matter? A collateral matter is one which is only relevant to the credit of the witness who is being cross-examined and to no other issue in the proceedings. Unfortunately, whether a matter is relevant to credit only is not always easy to determine. Thus, in *R. v. Hitchcock* (1847), the court proposed a test to determine whether a matter is collateral. The test is basically as follows. If the party who is cross-examining the witness could not have called evidence on the matter if the witness had not been called, because the matter is not relevant to an issue in the proceedings, the matter is collateral only and the witness's answer will be treated as final. If, on the other hand, the cross-examining party could have called evidence on the matter whether or not the witness had been called, because the matter is relevant to an issue in the proceedings, the matter is not collateral and the witness's answer will not be treated as final.

An example of a case in which a matter was treated as collateral in *R. v. Burke* (1858). A witness who had informed the court that he could not speak English was allowed to give his evidence through an interpreter. After he had done so, it was put to him in cross-examination that he had been heard speaking in English outside the court. This he denied and the court then had to determine whether his ability to speak English was a collateral matter, to which his answer would be treated as final. The court decided that, as the questioning related only to the witness's credit, it was collateral (the witness's knowledge of English not being an issue in the proceedings).

The exceptions to the rule regarding the finality of questions relating to collateral matters

(a) *Bias*. If a witness denies an allegation put to him during cross-examination that he is biased, although bias is a collateral matter, the cross-examination party may call evidence to prove the witness's bias. The following cases illustrate this exception.

In *R. v. Mendy* (1976), the accused's husband was asked during cross-examination whether he had, prior to testifying, and in an attempt to adapt his evidence, spoken to someone who had heard the testimony of the prosecution witnesses. The husband denied this allegation. The Court of Appeal upheld the trial judge's decision to allow the prosecution to call evidence in rebuttal.

In *R. v. Phillips* (1936) the accused was charged with incest. During cross-examination, his daughter (the alleged victim) and another daughter denied having been schooled by their mother into putting forward the allegation of incest. On appeal, the court held that the trial judge had been wrong in refusing to allow the defence to call evidence to rebut the daughters' denial.

In *R. v. Busby* (1982), an allegation was put during cross-examination that police officers were prepared to cheat in order to obtain a conviction—by fabricating evidence and threatening a defence witness. Although the court treated the questions as not being collateral but rather as relevant to an issue in the trial, the case has subsequently been interpreted (in *R. v. Edwards*, below) as one falling within the bias exception so that the defence ought to have been allowed to all evidence to rebut the officers' denial.

A similar case to *Busby*, but one which fell outside the exception, is *R. v. Edwards* (1991). The accused argued in his defence that the evidence against him had been fabricated. Police officers who testified for the prosecution were cross-examined as to whether their testimony in earlier trials, which had resulted in acquittals or quashed convictions due to fabrication of the evidence, had been untrue. The Court of Appeal held that because the issue was of the police officers' credibility in the present proceedings, the cross-examination related to a collateral matter but did not involve a suggestion of bias and, therefore, the officers' answers ought to be treated as final.

(b) *Previous inconsistent statements.* Questions put during cross-examination concerning previous inconsistent statements are collateral. The witness's answers to such questions will not be final, though, and a previous inconsistent statement can be adduced in rebuttal. The relevance of a previous statement adduced in this way depends on the nature of the proceedings. In criminal proceedings, it is relevant to credit only (see *R. v. Askew* (1981)) and in civil proceedings it is admissible as evidence of the truth of its factual content (see section 1 of the Civil Evidence Act 1995).

(c) *The previous convictions of a witness, other than the accused.* Section 6 of the Criminal Procedure Act 1865 has the effect that should a witness in either civil or criminal proceedings deny during cross-examination the existence of their previous convictions, cross-examining counsel may adduce evidence of those convictions in rebuttal.

(d) *Witness's reputation for untruthfulness.* A witness may be called to state that the other side's witness is generally known to be untruthful (see *R. v. Longman* (1968)).

(e) *Disability of witness.* A medical witness may be called to attack a witness's credibility on the basis of their inability to give truthful testimony due to their physical or mental disability (see *Toohey v. Metropolitan Police Commissioner* (1965)).

Cross-examination of the complainant in a rape offence case

How is the complainant in a rape offence case treated differently to other witnesses? As we have already seen, all witnesses may be cross-examined with a view to discrediting their testimony. Therefore, if a special rule did not exist to protect the alleged victim in a rape offence case, she could have her evidence attacked by allegations of promiscuity. Thus, the scope of permitted cross-examination of a complainant in a rape offence case has been limited by statute.

Section 2 of the Sexual Offences Amendment Act 1976 provides that the complainant in such a case may not be cross-examined about her sexual experience with anyone other than the accused except with the leave of the judge. Leave is also required before any other evidence relating to her sexual experience may be adduced.

Section 2 does not prevent cross-examination of the complainant about her sexual experience with the accused, nor does it prevent the complainant being examined in chief about her sexual experience with men other than the accused.

To which offences does section 2 apply? Section 2 applies to rape offences only. Rape offences are: rape; attempted rape; aiding, abetting, counselling or procuring rape or attempted rape. Where an accused is charged with a non-rape offence as well as a rape offence, section 2 will still apply but the judge can take into acount the existence of the non-rape offence(s) in deciding whether to grant leave (see *R. v. C* (1992)).

What does the term "sexual experience" mean? There is no definition of the term in the statute and it has been interpreted quite widely by the courts. Thus, it includes activities which fall short of sexual intercourse, for example physical advances and words used to suggest that the complainant is willing to engage in sexual intercourse or the presence in the complainant's flat in the morning of a man wearing only his slippers (see *R. v. Viola* (1982)).

In what circumstances will a judge grant leave for the defence to cross-examine the complainant about her sexual experience or to adduce such evidence by other means? Section 2(1) of the Sexual Offences (Amendment) Act provides that the judge may grant leave if he considers it would be unfair to the accused to refuse it. Guidance as to the circumstances in which it is likely to be unfair to the accused to refuse leave can be found in some of the reported cases in this area.

In *R. v. Lawrence* (1977), the court took the view that it would be unfair to refuse leave if the cross-examination could influence a reasonable jury to question the truth of the complainant's evidence.

In *R. v. Viola*, the court took the view that leave would rarely be allowed to ask questions relevant to credit only but leave was likely to be allowed if the questions were relevant to an issue in the case, for example, consent.

RE-EXAMINATION

This, the third and final stage of the examination of a witness, is the stage at which a witness who has been cross-examined may be re-examined by the party who called him. Re-examination is not essential but it does give the examining party an opportunity to ask about matters raised in cross-examination or, with the leave of the judge, any matters overlooked in examination in chief. As with examination in chief, leading questions may not be asked (see *Ireland v. Taylor* (1949)).

5. EVIDENCE OF OPINION

Primarily, witnesses are called to give evidence of facts which they have perceived and evidence of opinions which they have formed is not admissible. At times, however, the opinion evidence of a witness may be admissible because the opinion of that witness forms an issue before the court (*e.g.* the opinion of a person charged with handling stolen goods is admissible to prove that the accused believed the goods to be stolen—*R. v. Hulbert* (1979)). Moreover, for a variety of purposes, witnesses are permitted to give evidence of general reputation (for example, a character witness may give evidence of the general reputation of the accused in the neighbourhood where he lives—see *R. v. Rowton* below). The two major situations in which opinion evidence is commonly admitted, however, are, first, when a non-expert witness conveys facts which he has perceived to the court in terms of his opinion and, secondly, where an expert witness gives the court the benefit of his expert opinion in relation to a matter falling outside the experience of the court.

NON-EXPERT WITNESSES

In civil proceedings, where a non-expert witness conveys facts which he has perceived to the court in terms of his opinion, his statement of opinion is admissible as evidence of the facts which he perceived (Civil Evidence Act 1972, s 3(2)). It appears that the position in criminal cases is largely identical. Thus, in *R. v. Davies* (1962), it was proper for a witness to state his opinion to the effect that when he and the accused met, "the accused was under the influence of drink". It should be noted, however, that a non-expert witness cannot state his opinion upon a matter the formation of a proper opinion in respect of which requires expertise (see *R. v. Loake* (1911)). Moreover, a confession in the form of a statement of opinion may be worthless if its maker does not possess sufficient knowledge or expertise to make his opinion of some value (see *Bird v. Adams* (1972)).

Is there any difference between the position of the non-expert witness in civil and in criminal proceedings? If there is a significant distinction between the position of the non-expert in civil and in criminal proceedings it is that in proceedings of the latter type the non-expert may not be permitted to state his opinion upon an ultimate issue (*i.e.* one which the court is required to determine). Thus, for example, in *R. v. Davies*, in which the accused was charged with being unfit to drive through drink, the Court of Appeal held that a non-expert witness should not have been permitted to state that in his opinion the accused was "in no condition to handle a motor vehicle". In civil proceedings, the evidence of a non-expert witness upon an ultimate issue is admissible (Civil Evidence Act 1972 s.3(2)).

EXPERT WITNESSES

Essentially (and subject to the leave of the court being given where the party calling an expert fails to satisfy pre-trial disclosure requirements laid down by rules of court), the opinion evidence of an expert witness upon facts which have been proved by admissible evidence is admissible if it relates to a matter which falls outside the experience of the court.

When do rules of court require the disclosure of expert evidence in civil proceedings? A party to civil proceedings who wishes to adduce expert evidence must, unless the other parties agree to its admission, either comply with pre-trial disclosure requirements laid down by RSC, Ord. 38 or CCR, Ord. 20, or obtain the leave of the court. Since neither agreement nor leave may be forthcoming, the normal course of events is that a party either applies to the court for a direction on disclosure and complies with that direction or (where the relevant action is a personal injury action other than one brought in respect of medical negligence or an Admiralty action) complies with automatic directions laid down by RSC, Ord. 25 or CRR, Ord. 20.

Where a party applying for directions wishes to adduce oral expert evidence, the court will normally direct the party to disclose the evidence to the other parties in the form of a written report. The court may also direct that there be a meeting "without prejudice" of experts in order to identify which aspects of expert opinion are in dispute. The party who disclosed the expert report may put it in evidence but even if that party does not wish to do so, it may be put in evidence by a party to whom it was disclosed. Where a party applying for directions wishes to adduce written expert evidence and alleges that the expert cannot or should not be called, the court may direct that a modified version of the notice procedure contained in RSC, Ord. 38, rr. 20–23 (see Chapter 9 below) shall apply.

[*Note:* whilst reference is made in the course of this Chapter to the Supreme Court Rules and to the County Court Rules, it appears that, from April 1999, both sets of rules will be replaced by the Civil Procedure Rules. The new rules, which, unfortunately, were not available at the time of writing, will make significant changes in relation to the use of expert evidence in civil proceedings.]

When do rules of court require the disclosure of expert evidence in criminal proceedings? A party to criminal trial in the Crown Court who wishes to adduce expert evidence other than in relation to sentencing must either comply with pre-trial disclosure requirements laid down by the Crown Court (Advance Notice of Expert Evidence) Rules 1987 or obtain the leave of the court. Essentially, the rules require disclosure of a written statement of the expert's findings or opinions and also, but only where this is requested in writing by another party, both of the records of observations, tests, calculations or procedures which form the basis of such findings or opinions and of documents or things in respect of which such procedures were carried out. Where a party has reasonable grounds to believe that the disclosure of evidence under the 1987 Rules may lead either to the intimidation or attempted intimidation of one of that party's witnesses or, otherwise, to interference with the course of justice, however, then the party is not required to disclose the relevant evidence. Moreover, a party entitled to disclosure of a statement, record, etc., under the 1987 Rules may, in writing, waive his right to be furnished with it or may agree that the expert's findings and opinions will be furnished to him orally. The Magistrates' Courts (Advance Notice of Expert Evidence) Rules 1997 are of similar effect to the Crown Court

Rules except that the duty of disclosure only arises where the accused pleads not guilty.

How can an expert be identified? It is for the judge to determine the competence of a witness to give expert evidence. Clearly, factors such as qualifications, training and experience will all be relevant but, fundamentally, if, by virtue of his experiences, the witness has acquired the necessary expertise, the fact that he lacks formal qualifications and training does not prevent him from being competent to give expert evidence (see *R. v. Stockwell* (1993)). Where a witness is not an expert, however, then, as was noted above, the witness cannot state his opinion upon a matter the formation of a proper opinion in respect of which requires expertise.

Must the expert have personally perceived the facts upon which his opinion is based? Essentially, the facts in relation to which the opinion evidence of an expert is required must be proved by admissible evidence. Thus, it may be that the expert did himself perceive the relevant facts and can give evidence of them, in which case they may be proved by his evidence. Alternatively, where the expert did not himself perceive the relevant facts, it may be necessary to call another witness to prove them, the expert stating his opinion based upon the facts so proved. Thus, in *R. v. Abadom* (1983), an expert witness was by his own testimony able to prove that the refractive indices of two samples of glass were the same because he had personally analysed the samples. In contrast, in *R. v. Mason* (1911), an expert was only entitled to state his opinion as to whether wounds on a body which the expert had not examined were self-inflicted because a witness who had examined the body had been called to prove the relevant facts.

In forming his opinion, it may be that an expert does not merely consider the facts of the case with which he is concerned but also takes into account other information, such as that contained in specialist text books and articles. The expert may well have no personal knowledge of some or all of the information contained in these books or articles because, for example, they relate to scientific tests which he has not himself conducted or to phenomena which he has not personally perceived. Even so, the expert is entitled to take this information into account in forming his opinion (see *R. v. Abadom*). In *R. v. Abadom*, a scientist was required to determine whether broken glass found in the accused's shoe had come from a particular window. He determined and compared the refractive indices of the glass in the shoe and of glass from the window and found that they were the same. He also relied upon Home Office statistics which showed that only a small percentage of glass samples shared this refractive index. Thus, he concluded that there was strong evidence that the glass in the shoe had come from the window. The Court of Appeal held that the expert was entitled to rely upon the Home Office data.

[**Note**: now that the Civil Evidence Act 1995 is in force, experts in civil proceedings will generally be able to give hearsay evidence of relevant facts which they have not perceived, but the weight of such evidence may be limited (see Chapter 9 below).]

When does a matter fall outside the court's experience?

Expert evidence is admissible where a court is required to determine an issue which falls outside its experience. For example, if a jury is required to consider whether the accused could have killed the victim whilst the accused was sleepwalking, the jury is entitled to expert assistance, the capabilities of a sleepwalker being outside the experience of the average juror (see *R. v. Smith* (1979)). Equally, where a jury in reaching its verdict is required to take into account the characteristics of an accused who is said to be mentally ill or of sub-normal I.Q., the evidence of psychiatrists or psychologists may be admissible (see *R. v. Maish* (1986)).

In contrast, expert evidence is not admissible where the issue before the court is one which falls within the court's experience. Thus, for example, if a jury is required to consider whether it is likely that a normal person (*i.e.* one who is not mentally ill or of sub-normal I.Q.) would have been provoked in given circumstances, psychiatric advice is not required, and, consequently, is not admissible, the issue falling within the experience of the jury (*R. v. Turner* (1975)). Equally, it has been held that a jury does not require expert advice in order to determine whether a publication is obscene (see *R. v. Calder & Boyers* (1969)).

Fundamentally, however, whether a court requires the assistance of an expert will vary with the facts of each specific case. Thus, for example, whether a jury requires the assistance of a facial mapping expert in order to determine whether the man whose image was captured in a photograph is the man in the dock before them may depend upon factors such as whether the man in the photograph was wearing a disguise (see *R. v. Stockwell* (1993)). Consequently, in this context there may arise exceptional cases, determined on their own special facts, which subsequent courts are quick to distinguish as not establishing any general principles.

Two well known examples of such cases are *Lowery v. R.* 91974) and *DPP v. A. & B.C. Chewing Gum Ltd* (1968). In the former case, the evidence of a psychologist was held to be admissible for the defence of one of two co-defendants for the purpose of assisting the jury to determine which of the two co-defendants was the most likely to have committed a murder. The case was exceptional, one or other of the two accused (or both) must have been the killer, the killing lacked any motive other than sadism and each defendant asserted that the other had committed the murder. In the latter case, psychiatric evidence was properly admitted with regard to the issue whether a publication was obscure because, exceptionally, the question before the jury was not whether the relevant material was likely to corrupt or deprave an adult but rather was whether it was likely to corrupt or deprave a child. Both cases have subsequently been classified as exceptional by the Court of Appeal (see, respectively, *R. v. Turner* and *R. v. Anderson* (1972)).

Whose opinion is decisive—the court's or the expert's?

Where expert evidence is admissible, the expert does not, or should not, replace the tribunal of fact. Thus, for example, in a jury trial it should be the opinion of the jury, not the opinion of the expert which determines the relevant issue. It is for the jury to determine what weight should be given to the expert's evidence. Consequently, a jury should not normally be directed to accept the evidence of an expert (*R. v. Lanfear* (1968)). Indeed, it will often be that the jury are required to choose between the opinions of two or more experts, prosecution and defence. Exceptionally, however, it may be that in the absence of other evidence a jury should be directed to accept "unequivocal, uncontradicted" expert evidence (see *R. v. Sanders* (1991)). Certainly, a direction to a jury encouraging them to undervalue the evidence of an expert is equally improper (see *Anderson v. R.* (1972)).

Whilst it is for the tribunal of fact and not for the expert to determine the issues before the court, this does not prevent the expert from stating his opinion upon an ultimate issue provided that expert assistance is required. That this is so in civil proceedings is clearly established by reference to section 3(1) of the Civil Evidence Act 1972 (*Re M & R* (Minors) (1996)). So far as criminal proceedings are concerned, it appears that the position is, in practice, largely the same, though the jury must be reminded that it is for them, and not for the expert, to determine the relevant issue (*R. v. Stockwell*).

6. PRIVILEGE

In this Chapter we will consider the nature of three forms of privilege, namely, the privilege which attaches to communications made "without prejudice", the privilege against self-incrimination and legal professional privilege. Essentially, where a party is entitled to claim privilege and does so, he may be entitled to, or to require another to, refuse to answer questions in court, refuse to provide answers to interrogatories or refuse to produce documents sought by other parties during discovery. A party entitled to claim privilege may, however, waive it (*i.e.* relinquish the right to claim it).

COMMUNICATIONS MADE "WITHOUT PREJUDICE"

When does the privilege arise?

Essentially, a communication is privileged if made in the course of a genuine attempt to negotiate the settlement of an action, unless the communication is made upon an "open" basis. Thus, during an attempt to negotiate a settlement, a party may make an admission of liability safe in the knowledge that should the matter end up in court the admission cannot be put in evidence against him without his consent. Whilst it is normal and correct practice to head a letter written in the course of such negotiations "without prejudice", the presence or absence of such a heading is not decisive. Consequently, the fact that a letter is headed "without prejudice" does not, in itself, give rise to the privilege and, conversely, a letter written in the course of negotiations aimed at settlement may be privileged even though the "without prejudice" heading is missing and even though it is headed "open letter" (see *Dixon's Stores Group Ltd v. Thames Television plc* (1993)).

Does the privilege come to an end when settlement is reached and can it be claimed against a third party?

The privilege subsists even after a settlement has been reached and not only prevents the party to whom the privileged communication was made from making use of admissions contained therein against its maker but also prevents third parties from so doing (*Rush & Tompkins v. Greater London Council* (1989)). Thus, where A makes an admission in the course of negotiations with B which are aimed at the settlement of a dispute between them, the communication is privileged whether or not a settlement was eventually reached and, consequently, neither B nor C (a third party) can make use of the admission in litigation concerning its subject-matter. The parties to "without prejudice negotiations" may, however, jointly waive the privilege. Moreover, it appears that, in the context of litigation by a third party against one of the parties to the negotiations, the privilege may be waived by that party alone (*Muller v. Linsley & Mortimer (a Firm)* (1994)).

Exceptions and extension

The operation of the privilege is subject to a number of exceptions. For example, it does not prevent the admission of communications where the issue before the court is whether a settlement was reached (see *Walker v. Wilsher* (1889)). Conversely, it should be noted that the ambit of the privilege has been extended, in the context of matrimonial conciliation, to encompass mediation between parties by a mediator, such as a marriage guidance counsellor (see, for example, *Mole v. Mole* (1951)).

SELF-INCRIMINATION

When does the privilege arise?

Basically, a person is not required to answer a question (either in court or in the form of an interrogatory) or to produce a document sought by another party if answering the question or producing the document would tend to expose him to a criminal charge which is reasonably likely to be preferred or to a penalty or forfeiture which is reasonably likely to be sued for (see *Blunt v. Park Lane Hotel Ltd* (1942)). A person entitled to claim the privilege may, however, waive the right to do so.

[**Note:** an example of a penalty is one imposed by the Inland Revenue; an example of forfeiture is forfeiture of property under a lease.]

Statutory removal of the privilege

The right to claim the privilege has been removed by statute in a variety of contexts, both expressly and by necessary implication.

Thus, for example: where the accused chooses to testify in criminal proceedings, statute expressly provides that he may be asked questions tending to criminate him (Criminal Evidence Act 1898, s 1(e)).

Similarly, statute expressly provides that a person may be asked questions which may incriminate that person or his or her spouse or may be required to comply with an order of the court which is of the like effect in proceedings for the recovery or administration of property, for the execution of a trust or for an account of property or dealings therewith (Theft Act 1968, s 31). Where a person answers such a question or complies with such an order as required by section 31, however, the statements or admissions which the person makes are not admissible in evidence against the person or the spouse in subsequent proceedings for an offence under the Theft Act 1968 unless, in the case of the spouse, the marriage took place after the statements or admissions were made.

An example of the implied removal of the privilege by statute is provided by the examination of persons by inspectors appointed by the Department of Trade and Industry under the authority of the Companies Act 1985. Whilst the relevant statutory provisions do not expressly remove the privilege, if the privilege could be claimed by persons so examined this would prevent the attainment of the relevant statutory purpose (namely, the investigation of fraud—see *Bank of England v. Riley* (1992)).

[**Note:** where a statute expressly or impliedly removes the privilege against self-incrimination and does not provide an alternative protection (thus requiring a person, upon pain of punishment if he refuses to do so, to provide evidence which might be used in subsequent criminal proceedings against him), this appears to amount to a violation of Article 6 of the European Convention on Human Rights (*Saunders v. United Kingdom* (1996)).]

Judicial alternatives to the privilege

In recent years, the courts have demonstrated a willingness to order a person to disclose information, the production of which might ordinarily expose him to a criminal charge, where they have been able to ensure that the production of the relevant information would not be used against that person in subsequent criminal proceedings. Thus, for example, disclosure has properly been ordered subject to a condition that the information disclosed would not be used in criminal proceedings against the person required to dis-

close the relevant information. It appears, however, that such an
order should only be made where the prosecuting authority agrees
not to use the information so disclosed in criminal proceedings
against the person required to disclose it (*A.T. & T. Istel v. Tully*
(1993)).

When will a judge uphold a claim of privilege?

In determining whether the privilege applies, the judge must consider not merely whether the answer to a question or the production of a document would directly criminate the person answering
the question or producing the document but also whether it would
provide evidence which, in combination with other evidence, might
form the basis of a charge against that person (see *R. v. Slaney*
(1832); *R. v. Boyes* (1861)). Moreover, even if answering a question
or producing a document would either incriminate the person
answering the question or producing the document or provide evidence against that person, the judge will not uphold a claim of privilege if the possibility that a charge will be preferred is a remote on
such as would not influence the conduct of a reasonable man (see
R. v. Boyes). Further, it appears that where the person claiming
privilege is already exposed to the risk that criminal charges will
be preferred and that answering a question or producing a document will not increase that risk, the claim will not be upheld (*R. v.
Khan* (1982)).

Where the privilege has not been removed by statute, is its application in civil and in criminal proceedings identical?

A person can no longer claim the privilege in civil proceedings
merely because answering a question or producing a document
would tend to expose that person to a forfeiture (Civil Evidence
Act 1968, s.16(1)(a)). Moreover, in civil proceedings, a spouse may
refuse to answer a question or to produce a document if answering
the question or producing the document would tend to expose his
or her spouse to a charge or penalty (Civil Evidence Act 1968,
s.14(1)(b)). Further, in civil proceedings a person cannot claim the
privilege merely because answering a question or producing a document would expose that person to a charge or penalty under the
law of a foreign country (Civil Evidence Act 1968, s.14(1)(a)).

Whether, within the context of criminal proceedings, a spouse
can claim the privilege to prevent the incrimination of his or her
spouse and whether, within that context, exposure to a criminal

charge or a penalty under foreign law can give rise to the privilege has not been conclusively determined. It should be noted, however, that, in any event, a penalty imposed under the law of the European Communicy is imposed under domestic law, not under foreign law (see *Rio Tinto Zinc Corporation v. Westinghouse Electric Corporation* (1978)).

LEGAL PROFESSIONAL PRIVILEGE

When does the privilege arise?

Basically, a client is entitled to refuse to answer questions (either in court or in the form of interrogatories) or to produce documents sought by another party during discovery, and is also entitled to require his legal adviser to do the same, where the questions concern or the documents comprise confidential communications between the client and the legal adviser the purpose of which was to request or provide legal advice. Further, the privilege also extends to encompass questions or documents concerning or comprising confidential communications between the client or his legal adviser and third parties if the dominant purpose of the relevant communications was to provide the legal adviser with information to be used by him in making preparation on his client's behalf for pending or anticipated legal proceedings. In this latter case the client is also entitled to require the third party to refuse to answer the relevant question or produce the relevant document.

Must a lawyer-client relationship exist in order for the privilege to arise?

If a lawyer-client relationship does not exist, then the privilege will not arise. Thus, for example, if C asks L, his friend, for his confidential advice in respect of a legal matter, the advice given by L will not be privileged, even though L is a lawyer, if L does not give it in the course of performing his professional duties (see *Smith v. Daniel* (1875)).

Are all lawyer-client communications confidential?

Not all lawyer-client communications are confidential. For example, if a client retains a solicitor and informs the solicitor of his address for correspondence purposes, it appears that, in the normal course of events, the solicitor's knowledge of the client's address does not amount to a professional confidence. If, however, the client was hiding from the police at a secret location, the communication of the address by the client to the lawyer might well be confidential (see *ex parte Campbell* (1870)).

In order for the privilege to arise, is it necessary that litigation is pending or anticipated?

So far as confidential communications between lawyer and client are concerned, all that is necessary is that the purpose of the communications was to request or provide legal advice. It is not necessary that litigation was pending or anticipated. Thus, for example, communications between solicitor and client concerning the drafting of a lease by the solicitor for the client may be privileged (*Balabel v. Air India* (1988)).

As regards communications with third parties, however, such communications are only privileged if the dominant purpose of the communications was to provide the legal adviser with information to be used by him in making preparation on his client's behalf for pending or anticipated legal proceedings. In *Waugh v. British Railways Board* (1980) the relevant communication was a report concerning the details of a railway accident which had been prepared equally for the purpose of accident prevention and for the purpose of providing the Board's legal adviser with information which he required in the context of anticipated legal proceedings. Since informing the Board's legal adviser was not the dominant purpose of the two, the House of Lords held that the report was not privileged.

Can the privilege attach to pre-existing documents which the client subsequently sends to the lawyer or to the third party?

Where a document does not amount to a lawyer—client or lawyer—third party communication, the fact that it is sent to the lawyer or to the third party does not entitle the client to claim that it is privileged. Thus, if a client sends an invoice containing a sample of his handwriting to his solicitor and the solicitor sends the invoice to a handwriting expert, the client is not entitled to claim privilege in respect of the invoice (*R. v. King* (1983)).

Does the operation of the privilege prevent a witness of fact from giving evidence of facts which he has personally perceived?

Where a third party has perceived relevant facts, the fact that he has engaged in privileged communications with the lawyer or the client does not prevent him from being called as a witness by another party to the relevant legal proceedings. If the client asserts his privilege, the witness cannot give evidence as to the content of the privileged communications, but the existence of the privilege does not prevent the third party from giving evidence of the facts which he has perceived (see *Harmony Shipping Co. v. Saudi Europe* (1979)). Equally, it appears that where a lawyer himself perceives relevant facts as opposed to learning of them from a privileged communication, his knowledge of the relevant facts is not privileged (see *Lyell v. Kennedy* (1884)).

Where two clients jointly retain a common legal adviser, can one successfully claim privilege against the other in respect of communications between the clients and the legal adviser?

Where two clients jointly retain a legal adviser, either may claim that communications made to the lawyer in the capacity of their joint legal adviser are privileged as against third parties but neither may claim that such communications are privileged as against each other (see *Re Konigsberg* (1989)).

Can the client successfully claim privilege against another party who shares a common interest with him in the subject-matter of the privileged communication?

A client cannot successfully claim privilege against a person with whom the client shares a common interest in the subject-matter of the privileged communication. Thus, for example, trustees cannot maintain privilege against a beneficiary in respect of communications concerning a disposition of trust property (In *Re Postlethwaite* (1887)). They could, however, maintain privilege in such communications against third parties.

Can the right to claim legal professional privilege be waived?

Legal professional privilege can only be claimed or waived by the client. If the client chooses to claim privilege it cannot be waived by the legal adviser or the third party. Equally, where the client chooses to waive privilege, it cannot be claimed by the legal adviser or the third party. It should be noted, however, that the legal adviser, whilst acting in the capacity of the client's agent, may waive privilege on the client's behalf. Thus, if a solicitor, whilst acting on his client's behalf, discloses a privileged document to another party by mistake, this may amount to a waiver of privilege (see *Guiness Peat Properties Ltd v. Fitzroy Robinson Partnership* (1987)). Equally, if the client's barrister mistakenly reads out part of a privileged document in court, this, too, may amount to a waiver of privilege in the entire document (see *Great Atlantic Insurance v. Home Insurance* (1981)). Moreover, where, in the course of legal proceedings, privilege is waived by one party in a communication which concerns a particular transaction, this may result in the other party being entitled to disclosure of other communications concerning the same transaction (see *General Accident Fire and Life Assurance Corporation Ltd v. Tanter* (1984)). Similarly, where a former client sues his former solicitor in negligence, this may give rise to an implied waiver of privilege by the client in relation to lawyer-client communications concerning the transaction which forms the subject matter of the negligence proceedings (*Lillicrap v. Nalder* (1993)).

Where a party has obtained possession of copies of privileged documents can he use these as secondary evidence to prove the contents of the originals?

Essentially, where a party to legal proceedings obtains possession of copies of privileged documents, the party may use the copies as secondary evidence to prove the contents of the originals (see *Calcraft v. Guest* (1898)). It may be, however, that, before the secondary evidence is adduced, a court will be prepared to grant the party entitled to claim privilege an injunction preventing the party in possession of the copies from making use of them (see *Lord Ashburton v. Pape* (1913)).

Basically, it appears that a court will be prepared to grant an injunction preventing the use of secondary evidence to prove the contents of a privileged document if the party entitled to claim the privilege applies for the injunction before the copies have been adduced in evidence and provided that there is no reason why the court, in the exercise of its discretion, should refuse to grant an equitable remedy (see *Goddard v. Nationwide Building Society* (1987)).

In general, such an injunction will be granted even though the conduct of the party wishing to adduce the secondary evidence has been entirely proper. Where, however, the party entitled to claim privilege permitted the party wishing to adduce the secondary evidence to inspect the relevant document in the course of discovery, then the latter party is normally entitled to assume that there has been a waiver of privilege (*Guiness Peat Properties Ltd v. Fitzroy Robinson Partnership*). Exceptionally, however, even in these circumstances an injunction may be granted, for example, where inspection had been obtained by fraud or where the party obtaining inspection or his solicitors must have realised that they were only permitted to inspect the relevant document in consequence of an obvious mistake (*Guiness Peat Properties Ltd v. Fitzroy Robinson Partnership*).

[**Note:** it appears that an injunction will not be granted to prevent the prosecution from making use of secondary evidence in criminal proceedings (see *Butler v. Board of Trade* (1971)).]

Are there exceptional circumstances in which a claim of legal professional privilege cannot be maintained?

(1) Until recently, it was believed that a claim of legal professional privilege would not be upheld where a defendant to criminal proceedings established on a balance of probabilities that the person claiming privilege no longer had an interest to protect and that the defendant did have a legitimate interest in adducing the privileged information in evidence. The House of Lords has now made clear, however, that a court cannot order the disclosure of privileged information in such circumstances, it being for the party entitled to claim the privilege to decide whether he wishes to waive it (*R. v. Derby Magistrates' Court, ex parte B* (1995)).

(2) It appears that a party may not be entitled to claim legal professional privilege arising from confidential communications between lawyer or client and third party either in the context of wardship proceedings or in the context of proceedings under the Children Act 1989 (see, respectively, *Re A* (1991) and *Re L (a minor)* (1996)).

(3) It appears that where the purpose of confidential communications was to facilitate the commission of criminal or fraudulent activity, the client cannot maintain the privilege even though neither the legal adviser nor the client were aware of the criminal or

fraudulent purpose (*R. v. Central Criminal Court, ex parte Francis and Francis* (1989)).

(4) Exceptionally, the privilege may be removed by statute (see *Jones v. Searle* (1978)).

---

7. ESTOPPEL BY RECORD AND THE USE OF PREVIOUS CONVICTIONS AND JUDICIAL FINDINGS AS EVIDENCE OF THE FACTS UPON WHICH THEY WERE BASED

In this Chapter we will consider both the operation of the doctrine of *res judicata* (estoppel by record) in civil and criminal proceedings and the extent to which previous convictions and judicial findings in civil cases may be adduced as evidence of the facts upon which they were based in proceedings between parties other than the parties to the proceedings in which the accused was convicted or the findings were made.

THE DOCTRINE OF *RES JUDICATA* IN CIVIL PROCEEDINGS

Is the judgment of a civil court conclusive evidence against all persons of the facts upon which it was based?

The judgment of a civil court is conclusive evidence against all persons of "the state of things which it actually effects" but not of the findings on which it is based (see *Hollington v. Hewthorn* (1943)). Thus, for example, if a court awards P £10,000 damages against D in consequence of D's breach of contract, the judgment conclusively proves that P was awarded £10,000 damages against D but does not conclusively prove that D breached his contract with P.

Where the judgment of a civil court does not merely determine the interests of the parties to it (*i.e.* whether one is liable in damages for breach of contract or in negligence to the other) but determines the "status" of a person or thing, however, then such status is determined conclusively as against all persons. For example, a decree of nullity is conclusive evidence against all persons of the invalidity of the relevant marriage (*Salvesen v. The Administrator of*

Austrian Property (1927)). A judgment of the former type is termed a judgment *in personam*. A judgment of the latter type is termed a judgment *in rem*.

Are parties to civil proceedings ever estopped from re-litigating findings made by a court in the course of civil proceedings between them?

A party to civil proceedings or his privies may be estopped from re-litigating findings made by a court in the course of civil proceedings between himself or his privies and another party or his privies. This form of estoppel is known as estoppel by record or estopped *per rem judicatam* and, as is the case with estoppels generally, will only take effect if pleaded (*Vooght v. Winch* (1819)). Such an estoppel may either take the form of a cause of action estoppel (preventing the re-litigation of a previously litigated cause of action) or that of an issue estoppel (preventing the re-litigation of an issue which formed an essential element of a previously litigated cause of action).

Thus, where P successfully sued D, a builder, for damages in respect of D's breach of a contract to complete a building in a "good and workmanlike manner", P could not, by bringing subsequent proceedings in respect of the same cause of action against D, recover further damages arising from consequences of D's defective workmanship which P had not particularised for the purposes of the original action (*Conquer v. Boot* (1928)).

Again, where, in legal proceedings brought by P's passenger T, P and D had been found equally liable in negligence in respect of the car crash in which T had been injured, P was, in the course of subsequent proceedings brought by P against D, estopped (an issue estoppel) from asserting other than that he was fifty per cent contributorily negligent, the issue having been determined in the course of the proceedings brought by T (*Wall v. Radford* (1991)).

What conditions must be satisfied in order for a cause of action estoppel or an issue estoppel to arise?

A cause of action estoppel or an issue estoppel may arise only if the following requirements are satisfied:

(1) The parties to the latter proceedings must be (or be the privies of) the parties to the original proceedings.

Thus, P was not estopped from denying contributory negligence

in an action which he brought against D concerning injuries which
P had suffered in a vehicle collision even though D had previously
proved contributory negligence in an action brought against D by
P's father, who owned the car which P had been driving, in respect
of the damage to his car (*Townsend v. Bishop* (1939)).

[*Note*: at the time when Townsend's case was decided, contributory negligence provided a complete defence to liability and consequently had P been estopped from denying contributory negligence his action must have failed.]

(2) The parties to the latter proceedings must be litigating in the
same capacities in which they litigated the original proceedings.

Thus, where, in legal proceedings brought by T, P and D had
been found equally to blame for a collision between vehicles in
which T's property had been damaged, P, litigating in the capacity
of personal representative of his wife (who had been killed in the
collision), was not estopped, in the course of subsequent proceedings against D, from denying contributory negligence (*Marginson
v. Blackburn B.C.* (1939)). P was, however, estopped from denying
contributory negligence when litigating on his own behalf.

[*Note*: at the time when Marginson's case was decided, contributory negligence provided a complete defence to liability and consequently the effect of the estoppel was that P could not bring his
personal action against D though he could bring the action on
behalf of his wife's estate.]

(3) The cause of action or issue which is being litigated in the latter
proceedings must have been determined in the original proceedings.

In *Wall v. Radford* (considered above), Popplewell J. held that, for
the purpose of determining whether P was estopped from denying
that he was 50 per cent contributorily negligent, the factual issues
raised in the subsequent proceedings were the same as those which
had been determined in the original proceedings. His Lordship
declined to follow earlier authority to the effect that where the subsequent proceedings involve consideration of legal duties of care different from those which the original proceedings concerned, the
issues raised in the subsequent proceedings are not the same as those
determined in the earlier proceedings (see *Bell v. Holmes* (1956)).

[*Note*: in exceptional circumstances a party may not be pre-
vented, by issue estoppel, from re-opening a previously litigated
issue. Such circumstances include those in which new evidence has

become admissible which could not, by exercising reasonable diligence, have been adduced in the original proceedings and those in which, following the original proceedings, there has been a change in the law (*Arnold v. National Westminster Bank* (1991)).]

In *Conquer v. Boot* (considered above), the plaintiff was debarred from bringing a second action in respect of the same cause of action. In contrast, in *Brunsden v. Humphrey* (1884), a cab driver was not debarred from bringing an action to recover damages for personal injuries which he had sustained in an accident by virtue of the fact that he had already recovered damages from the same defendant in earlier proceedings concerning damage to his cab resulting from the same accident. This was so as the two actions concerned two distinct causes of action.

(4) The court which determined the relevant issue in the original proceedings must have been a court of competent jurisdiction and must have given a final judgment upon the merits.

The decision of a court of tribunal which does not determine a dispute between contending parties cannot become conclusive evidence of the facts upon which it was based against the parties to subsequent civil proceedings, the court or tribunal not being a "court of competent jurisdiction" (see *The European Gateway* (1987)). Moreover, even where the decision of a court or tribunal does determine a dispute between contending parties, its decision will not become conclusive evidence of the facts upon which it was based against the parties to subsequent civil proceedings if the court or tribunal did not possess jurisdiction to finally determine the relevant issue (see *R. v. Hutchings* (1881)).

[**Note:** the fact that it is possible to appeal from the decision of a court or tribunal does not prevent its decision from being final for this purpose.]

Should a party to legal proceedings pursue every cause of action available to him?

If a party to legal proceedings does not pursue a cause of action which, exercising reasonable diligence, he might have pursued, it may be an abuse of process to attempt to pursue the cause of action in the course of subsequent proceedings between the same parties or their privies (*Henderson v. Henderson* (1843); *Talbot v. Berkshire County Council* (1994)). It should be noted, however, that the operation of this principle may not prevent a cause of action from being pursued in "special circumstances" (*e.g.* where one party did not pursue a cause of action in the original proceedings under an agreement with the other party or in reliance upon a representation made thereby (*Talbot v. Berkshire County Council*).

[*Note:* It appears that this principle is applicable, in the personal injuries context, to facts such as those of *Brunsden and Humphrey* and *Wall v. Radford*. Consequently, such proceedings may be struck out as an abuse of process (see *Talbot v. Berkshire County Council*)]

THE ADMISSIBILITY OF PREVIOUS CONVICTIONS AND JUDICIAL FINDINGS AS EVIDENCE OF THE FACTS UPON WHICH THEY WERE BASED IN CIVIL PROCEEDINGS BETWEEN PARTIES OTHER THAN THE PARTIES TO THE PROCEEDINGS IN WHICH THE ACCUSED WAS CONVICTED OR THE FINDINGS WERE MADE

The effect of the decision of the Court of Appeal in *Hollington v. Hewthorn* (1943) was that previous convictions and judicial findings were not admissible as evidence of the facts upon which they were based in civil proceedings between parties other than the parties to the proceedings in which the accused was convicted or the findings were made. Thus, in *Hollington v. Hewthorn*, in which P's car was damaged in a collision with a car driven by D, P was not entitled to adduce evidence of D's previous conviction for careless driving as evidence of D's negligence. The ambit of the rule in *Hollington v. Hewthorn* in civil proceedings has, however, been substantially reduced by sections 11, 12 and 13 of the Civil Evidence Act 1968.

The admissibility of previous convictions in civil proceedings

Essentially, section 11(1) of the Civil Evidence Act 1968 provides that a person's subsisting conviction is admissible in civil proceedings to prove that the person committed the offence of which he was convicted provided that proving that the relevant person committed the relevant offence is relevant to an issue before the court. The section also provides that where a person's conviction is admitted under the section, then the person shall be taken to have committed the offence of which he was convicted unless the contrary is proved.

[*Note:* a conviction is subsisting unless and until it has been quashed—*Re Raphael* (1973).]

Thus, were the facts of *Hollington v. Hewthorn* to arise today, D's conviction would not merely be admissible as evidence of his negli-

gence but, moreover, D would be presumed to have driven care-
lessly unless he proved that he had not done so. What is unclear,
however, is whether the effect of section 11 is merely to place the
burden of proving that he did not commit the offence on D or
whether, additionally, a conviction which is admitted under section
11 acts as evidence proving that D did, in fact, commit the relevant
offence (see *Stupple v. Royal Insurance Co Ltd* (1971)). Whichever
view is correct, it does appear that the task of rebutting the pre-
sumption that the person convicted of an offence in fact committed
it is, in general, not an easy one to accomplish (see *Hunter v. Chief
Constable of the West Midlands Police* (1982) A.C. 529).

[**Note:** where a party intends to adduce evidence of a previous
conviction under section 11 in High Court Proceedings he must
include a statement of such intent in his pleadings and if the other
party denies the conviction he must make the denial in his
pleadings—RSC, Ord. 18, r.7(A) (there is no longer such a requirement in relation to proceedings in the county court). Note, also,
that a certified copy of the certificate of conviction is admissible as
evidence of the conviction (section 11(4)).]

Finally, it should be noted that where the commission of a criminal offence by the plaintiff is relevant to an issue in proceedings for
libel or slander, the plaintiff's subsisting conviction for the relevant
offence is, under section 13 of the Civil Evidence Act 1968, admissible as *conclusive evidence* that he committed it.

The admissibility of previous findings of adultery and paternity in civil proceedings

Essentially, section 12 of the Civil Evidence Act 1968 provides that
subsisting findings of adultery made in matrimonial proceedings in
the High Court or in a County Court, subsisting findings of paternity and subsisting adjudications of paternity in affiliation proceedings are admissible in civil proceedings as evidence of adultery or
paternity provided that proving that the relevant person committed
the relevant adultery or fathered the relevant child is relevant to
an issue before the court. The section also provides that where a
finding or adjudication is admitted under the section then the
person who was found guilty of the relevant adultery or was found
to be the father of the relevant child shall be taken to have committed the relevant adultery or to have fathered the relevant child
unless the contrary is proved.

THE DOCTRINE OF *RES JUDICATA* IN CRIMINAL PROCEEDINGS

Can a person who has been convicted or acquitted of a criminal offence be subsequently tried for that offence?

A person who has been convicted of a criminal offence may plead *autrefois convict* in order to bar subsequent proceedings for the same offence against him. Similarly, a person who has been acquitted of a criminal offence may plead *autrefois acquit* in order to bar subsequent proceedings for the same offence against him. Further, the pleas of *autrefois convict* and *autrefois acquit* also bar proceedings against a person in respect of offences of which he could have been convicted on a previous indictment even if the relevant charge was not brought.

[**Note:** for an authoritative statement of these principles see *DPP v. Connelly* (1964) and *R. v. Beedie* (1997).]

In circumstances in which it is not possible to plead *autrefois convict* or *autrefois acquit*, can the doctrine of *res judicata* apply in criminal proceedings?

Where the accused has been acquitted of a criminal offence, the prosecution may not dispute his innocence of that offence in subsequent criminal proceedings. Thus, in *Sambasivam v. Malaya Federation Public Prosecutor* (1950), the accused's conviction for carrying a firearm was quashed because a statement had been admitted during his trial to the effect that he had both carried a firearm and been in possession of ammunition, the accused having previously been found not guilty of possessing the relevant ammunition.

Thus, where in proceedings against an accused the prosecution wish to rely upon evidence which was relied upon by the prosecution in earlier proceedings in which the accused was acquitted, it appears that they are only entitled to do so if, without the prosecution alleging that the accused was guilty of the offence of which he was acquitted or relying upon the drawing of such an inference by the jury, the evidence from the earlier proceedings is relevant to an issue in the later proceedings (see *G (An Infant) v. Coltart* (1967)).

Can an issue estoppel lie in criminal proceedings?

In *R. v. Humphreys* (1977) the House of Lords held that an issue estoppel cannot lie in criminal proceedings. Thus, during

Humphrey's trial for perjury, a police officer was
ted to testify that he had seen Humphreys di
vehicle in 1972 even though the police officer h₂
testified to the same effect during a trial at the en₍
Humphreys was acquitted of driving a motor vehicle w
qualified.

THE ADMISSIBILITY OF PREVIOUS CONVICTIONS AS EVIDENCE OF THE FACTS UPON WHICH THEY WERE BASED IN CRIMINAL PROCEEDINGS BETWEEN PARTIES OTHER THAN THE PARTIES TO THE PROCEEDINGS IN WHICH THE ACCUSED WAS CONVICTED

The ambit of the rule in _Hollington v. Hewthorn_ (see above) in criminal proceedings has been reduced by section 74 of the Police and Criminal Evidence Act 1984. Essentially, section 74(1) provides that a person's previous conviction is admissible in criminal proceedings in which he is not the accused to prove that the person committed the offence of which he was convicted provided that proving that the relevant person committed the relevant offence is relevant to an issue before the court. Section 74(2) provides that where a conviction is admitted under the section, then the relevant person shall be taken to have committed the offence of which he was convicted unless the contrary is proved.

[**Note:** the conviction must be a subsisting conviction, _i.e._ one which has not been quashed—_R. v. Golder_ (1987).]

A conviction may be admissible under section 74(1) either where it is relevant to an issue which forms an element of the offence with which the accused is charged (_e.g._ to prove that goods which the accused is alleged to have handled were stolen) or where it is relevant to a less fundamental issue, such as an evidential issue (_R. v. Robertson_ (1987)). Where a conviction is so relevant, however, the trial judge may well find it necessary to exclude it in the exercise of his discretion under section 78 of the 1984 Act upon the basis that its admission would have such an adverse effect on the fairness of the proceedings that it ought not to be admitted (_R. v. O'Connor_ (1987)). Moreover, where a conviction is admitted under section 74, the judge should explain to the jury why it has been admitted (_R. v. Kempster_ (1990)).

Finally, section 74(3) essentially provides that where the previous convictions of the accused are admissible in evidence (see Chapters 12 and 13 below), he shall be taken to have committed the relevant offences unless the contrary is proved.

8. THE RULE AGAINST HEARSAY: THE COMMON LAW

THE HEARSAY RULE

Basically, the effect of the rule against hearsay is that a statement is only admissible in legal proceedings as evidence of the truth of its factual content if it was made by a witness whilst testifying in those proceedings. The rule is, however, subject to a large number of exceptions, both common law and statutory. The statutory exceptions are examined in the course of the following three chapters. The purpose of this chapter is to consider both the nature of those statements which fall within the rule and the nature of its major common law exceptions.

To what types of statement does the hearsay rule apply?

The hearsay rule applies to written statements (including certain computer printouts), oral statements and statements made by conduct, and applies whether the relevant statement was made expressly or by implication, provided that two conditions are satisfied.

(1) The purpose for which the statement is tendered by the party wishing to rely upon it must be that of proving the truth of matters which the statement expressly or impliedly asserts to be true.
(2) The statement must have been made either out of court or in the course of legal proceedings other than those in which it is now being tendered.

Written statements For example, the hearsay rule applied where the prosecution, in order to identify certain cars, wished to rely upon written records kept by a car manufacturer which identified the cars by reference to numbers on their engines (*Myers v. DPP* (1965)). Consequently, the records were not admissible in evidence.

[*Note*: such records would now be admissible in evidence both in civil and in criminal proceedings under statutory exceptions to the hearsay rule; see Chapters 9 and 11 below.]

Oral statements For example, the hearsay rule applied where the prosecution, in order to prove that the accused had murdered the deceased, wished to rely on an oral statement made by the deceased shortly after he was attacked in which he named his attackers (*R. v. Andrews* (1987)).

[*Note*: the statement was admissible under an exception to the hearsay rule which is considered in the course of the present Chapter.]

Statements made by conduct For example, the hearsay rule applied where the prosecution, in order to prove that the accused had murdered the deceased, wished to rely upon a statement made by the deceased by gesture after her throat had been cut by which she identified the accused as the man who had cut her throat (*Chandrasekera v. R.* (1937)).

[*Note*: the statement was admissible under an exception to the hearsay rule.]

Implied statements For example, the hearsay rule applied where the prosecution, in order to prove that the accused dealt in drugs, wished to rely upon statements made by telephone to the accused's house asking both for him and for drugs (*R. v. Kearley* (1992)).

[*Note*: the House of Lords was of the view that the statements did not imply that the accused dealt in drugs and, consequently, were irrelevant and therefore inadmissible. Their Lordships accepted, however, that if the statements did imply that the accused dealt in drugs then they were still inadmissible as falling within the hearsay rule.]

Statements made in other legal proceedings For example, the hearsay rule applied to prevent the admission in subsequent legal proceedings as evidence of the place of a pauper's last legal settlement of a written and signed examination of the pauper, the pauper having been examined in court several years earlier for the purpose of determining the place of his last legal settlement (*R. v. The Inhabitants of Eriswell* (1790)).

[*Note*: statements made by witnesses in earlier legal proceedings may now be admissible under statutory exceptions to the hearsay rule.]

Computer printouts which fall within the hearsay rule

The hearsay rule applies to printouts produced by computers if information provided by a human source has been utilised in their production. This is so even where such information is stored by the machine and is subsequently utilised in the production of the printout (see, for example, *R. v. Coventry Justices, ex parte Bullard* (1992), in which printouts of poll tax records were held to fall within the hearsay rule, the relevant data having previously been inputted into the system by humans).

[*Note*: as is seen in Chapters 9 and 11 below, computer printouts which fall within the ambit of the hearsay rule may be admissible in civil and criminal proceedings under statutory exceptions to that rule.]

To what types of statement does the hearsay rule not apply?

The purpose for which the statement is tendered

The hearsay rule does not apply where the purpose for which the statement is tendered by the party wishing to rely upon it is other than that of proving the truth of matters which the statement expressly or impliedly asserts to be true. Thus, for example, the rule did not apply where the accused, whose defence was duress, wished to repeat in court threats made to him by terrorists (*Subramanian v. Public Prosecutor* (1956)). The rule did not apply because, in the context of the defence of duress, the statements were relevant regardless of whether they were true (in the sense that the terrorists actually intended to carry out the threats which they made) or false (in the sense that the terrorists had lied to the accused and did not intend to carry out the threats). Rather, what was important in that context was whether the threats had been made (which depended upon the truth of the accused's testimony in court and not upon that of the terrorist's statements). This was so because if the threats had been made and believed by the accused, they were potentially capable of amounting to duress whether or not there was, in reality, any intention to carry them out.

Computer printouts which do not fall within the hearsay rule The hearsay rule does not apply to printouts produced by machines which are used as mere tools, such as a computer which is used to perform a calculation (*R. v. Wood* (1982)). Equally, the rule does not apply to printouts produced by computers if information provided by a human source has not been utilised in their production. Thus, for example, printouts from a computer which recorded details of telephone calls (including the number called and the date and time of the conversation—*R. v. Spiby* (1990)) did not fall within the hearsay rule. It should be noted, however, that, contrary to the view of the Court of Appeal in *R. v. Spiby*, the House of Lords in *R. v. Shephard* (1993) held that the requirements of section 69 of the Police and Criminal Evidence Act 1984 (examined in Chapter 11 below) apply to computer produced documents whether or not the statements which they contain fall within the hearsay rule.

Photographs, video recordings, sketches and photofits It is clear that the hearsay rule does not apply to photographs or video-recordings of persons, places or events (see for example, *Taylor v. Chief Constable of Cheshire* (1987)). Further, it has been held that the hearsay rule does not apply to sketches and photofits of the perpetrators of criminal offences produced from information provided by witnesses (*R. v. Cook* (1987)). The basis of this latter decision is that sketches and photofits fall within the same class of evidence as photographs and that the production of a sketch or photofit effectively equates with the operation of a camera.

Matters not recorded Finally, it has been held that where a person responsible for the compilation and custody of records is called to prove that they are kept and compiled in such a way that if a matter is not recorded in them then it did not occur, the records do not fall within the hearsay rule if put in evidence for the purpose of proving that something which was not recorded in them did not occur (see *R. v. Shone* (1983)). The validity of this principle is, however, subject to some doubt (see *R. v. Coventry Justices, ex parte Bullard*).

MAJOR COMMON LAW EXCEPTIONS TO THE HEARSAY RULE

[**Note:** following the decision of the House of Lords in *Myers v. DPP*, the courts will no longer create new common law exceptions to the hearsay rule; the creation of new exceptions is now exclusively a task for Parliament.]

Dying declarations

[*Note*: this common law hearsay exception only applies in criminal proceedings for the murder or manslaughter of the person who made the hearsay statement.]

A statement made by a deceased person as to the cause of his death is admissible as evidence of the cause of his death if, when he made the statement, the deceased was under a settled hopeless expectation of death (*R. v. Perry* (1909)). If the deceased was under a settled hopeless expectation of death when he made the satatement, the fact that he subsequently began to believe that he might survive (*R. v. Austin* (1912)) or that he survived for several weeks after making it (*R. v. Bernadotti* (1869)) does not render it inadmissible. If, however, when he made the statement, the deceased believed that he would or might recover, then the exception does not apply (see *R. v. Hayward* (1833)). Moreover, the exception does not apply if the person who made the statement would not have been a competent witness at the time when he made it (*R. v. Pike* (1829)).

Finally, it should be noted that where a dying declaration is admitted, the judge should direct the jury to scrutinise the evidence with care (*Nembhard v. R.* (1981)).

Statements forming part of the *res gestae*

[*Note*: it appears that these common law hearsay exceptions apply only in criminal proceedings as they have not been preserved by section 7 of the Civil Evidence Act 1995 (see Chapter 9 below).]

Statements which are closely associated with an act or state of affairs the performance or existence of which is of relevance in legal proceedings may be admissible in those proceedings as evidence of the truth of their factual content. Essentially, a statement may be so admissible either if it concerns its maker's contemporaneous actions, physical sensations or state of mind or if it is closely associated with a dramatic event.

Statements concerning the contemporaneous actions, physical sensations or state of mind of their maker A statement explaining its maker's actions which was made at the time when the relevant actions were performed may be admissible to prove why they were performed. Thus, if a person, whilst away from home, writes a letter explaining why he is staying away from home, the letter may be admissible to prove why he stayed away from home, should this be of relevance to an issue before the court (see *Rouch v. Great Western Railway Co* (1841)). Moreover, it has been held that where a witness cannot remember whom he identified at an identification parade, a police officer who attended the parade can repeat in court the statement which the witness made at the time identifying the accused, the statement accompanying and explaining the activities of seeing and recognising (*R. v. McKay* (1990)).

A statement concerning its maker's physical sensations which was made at the time when he experienced the relevant sensations is admissible to prove that he experienced the relevant sensations but is not admissible as evidence of their cause. Thus, if a patient, whilst being examined by a doctor, tells the doctor that he has a pain in his leg and also tells the doctor that the pain was caused by an insect sting, the doctor may repeat the statement in court for the purpose of proving that the patient was in pain but may not do so for the purpose of proving that the patient had been stung by an insect (see *Amys v. Barton* (1911)). Moreover, where a patient is ill for several days, a statement made several days into the period of illness may be admissible to prove that the illness had been on-going from the date of its commencement (*Aveson v. Lord Kinnaird* (1805)).

Finally, a statement concerning its maker's state of mind at the time when he made the statement is admissible to prove what its maker intended to do or believed to be the case at that time but is not admissible as evidence of the truth of its maker's beliefs. Thus, where a man states that he is insolvent, his statement may be repeated in court to prove that he was aware of his insolvency but the fact of his insolvency must be proved by other admissible evidence (see *Thomas v. Connell* (1838)).

A statement of intent may be admissible whether it was made at the time when the intended act was carried out or whether it was made prior to performance of that act, in which case the court may be entitled to infer that the intent was still possessed by the maker at the relevant time (see *R. v. Moghal* (1977)). The longer the time gap between the making of the statement and the performance of the act, however, the lower the probative value of the statement, if it is admitted in evidence, will be. Moreover, if the statement was made after the performance of the relevant act, a court will be unlikely to admit it if the time gap was substantial (see *R. v. Moghal*).

[*Note:* it is unclear whether a statement of intent may be admitted in evidence to prove that the act which its maker intended to perform was, in fact, carried out by him. There is authority both for and against his proposition (see, respectively, *R. v. Buckley* (1873) and *R. v. Wainwright* (1875). It is also unclear whether statements concerning their maker's state of mind are admissible because they fall within a common law exception to the hearsay rule or whether such statements are not hearsay statements at all (see, for example, *R. v. Gilfoyle* (1996)).]

Statements closely associated with a dramatic event Statements closely associated with a dramatic event are admissible as evidence of the truth of their factual content if the possibility that they have been concocted or distorted can be disregarded. As the House of Lords made clear in *R. v. Andrews* (1987), the judge must determine whether this is so by considering whether the maker's mind was so dominated by the event at the time when the statement was made that the possibility of concoction or distortion can be ruled out. The judge must take into account any factors which might increase the risk of concoction or distortion, such as whether the maker had a motive to concoct or distort. Moreover, the judge should consider any factors which give rise to a particular risk of error. For example, where the statement relates to an identification which the maker made, it may be that the identification was made in circumstances in which the reliability of identification evidence would be doubtful (*e.g.* a fleeting glimpse of a person a long way away in the dark). Finally, if the judge decides that the statement is admissible, he should still draw the jury's attention to factors which might increase the risk of concoction or distortion or which might give rise to a particular risk of error and direct them that they must be satisfied that there was no concoction or distortion.

In Andrew's case, the question before the House of Lords was whether a statement made by a murder victim identifying the accused as the murderer had properly been admitted in evidence. The statement had been made by Andrews a few minutes after he was fatally stabbed. The statement had been admitted by the trial judge even though there was evidence to suggest that Andrews had a motive to concoct evidence against the accused and even though the possibility of error was increased because Andrews had been drinking heavily. The House of Lords held that, upon the facts of the case, the trial judge had been entitled to decide that there was no possibility of concoction or distortion and, consequently, that the evidence had properly been admitted.

In order for a statement to be admitted under this exception to the hearsay rule, it is necessary that the existence of the dramatic event and that the statement was made in its context are both proved by evidence other than the content of the statement itself (*Rattan v. R.* (1972)). Where, for example, the relevant statement was a request for the police made to a telephone operator by an hysterical woman, the Privy Council held that evidence that the statement was closely associated with a dramatic event was provided by the fact that the accused's wife had been shot and killed in the house from which the call was made a few minutes after it was made, by the fact that she made the statement in a call requesting the police and by her tone of voice when she made the call (*Rattan v. R.*).

[**Note:** a statement may be admitted under this exception to the hearsay rule whether it was made by the victim of a crime, by a third party or even by the accused (see *R. v. Glover* (1991)).]

---

9. CIVIL EVIDENCE ACT 1995

The Civil Evidence Act 1995 provides a statutory regime which makes hearsay evidence admissible in civil proceedings. The effect of the definition of "civil proceedings" in section 11 is, however, that the provisions of the Act do not apply to Civil proceedings to which the strict rules of evidence are inapplicable (*e.g.* arbitration before a county court). Moreover, the Act does not apply to proceedings begun before January 31, 1997 (*Bairstow and Others v. Queens Moat Houses plc* (1997)).

[**Note:** whilst reference is made in the course of this Chapter to the Supreme Court Rules and to the County Court Rules, it appears that, from April 1999, both sets of rules will be replaced by the Civil Procedure Rules which, unfortunately, were not available at the time of writing.]

ADMISSIBILITY

Section 1 of the Civil Evidence Act 1995 makes hearsay evidence admissible in civil proceedings. Moreover, this is so whether hearsay evidence takes the form of evidence of fact or evidence of opinion (see the definition of "statement" in section 13). Section 14 provides, however, that section 1 does not make hearsay evidence admissible if the hearsay evidence is inadmissible for some reason other than its hearsay nature (*e.g.* if it is inadmissible due to the operation of some other rule of evidence, of some other statutory provision or rules of court). Thus, for example, hearsay evidence in the form of a representation of opinion will only be admissible if the rules concerning the admission of opinion evidence have been complied with (see Chapter 5 above).

Section 1 also provides that sections 2 to 6 of the 1995 Act (considered below) do not apply where hearsay evidence is admissible under some exception to the hearsay rule other than the general exception provided by section 1 (*e.g.* under a common law exception to the hearsay rule preserved by section 7, (considered below), or under an exception to the hearsay rule provided by some other statutory provision).

Hearsay notices

Section 2 of the Civil Evidence Act 1995 and the rules of court made under it (RSC, Ord. 38, rr.20–24 and CCR, Ord. 20, rr.14–17) require a party intending to adduce hearsay evidence in civil proceedings to serve a hearsay notice on the other parties to the proceedings and, if requested, to provide the other parties with further information concerning the hearsay evidence. The parties may, however, agree to dispense with the requirements of section 2 and a party entitled to receive a hearsay notice, etc., may waive his entitlement. Moreover, section 2 only requires a party to comply with its requirements to the extent to which, in the circumstances, such compliance is reasonable and practicable in order to enable the other parties to deal with the relevant evidence in consequence of its hearsay nature. Further, it should be noted that the requirements of section 2 do not apply either in relation to affidavit evidence or in relation to statements allegedly made by persons whose estates form the subject matter of probate actions.

A hearsay notice should identify the hearsay statement(s) to which it relates and the maker(s) thereof, should indicate why the maker(s) will not testify and, where a hearsay statement is to be proved by the testimony of a witness, should indicate in which part of the witness's witness statement the hearsay evidence is contained. Essentially, a hearsay notice should be served at the same time as service of witness statements (where witness statements are not served, rules of court make specific provision concerning the time period within which hearsay notices must be served).

Where a party fails to comply with the requirements of section 2 **this does not affect the admissibility of the hearsay evidence.** Such failure may, however, be taken into account by the court when determining the weight of the hearsay evidence, may result in an adjournment and may be of relevance when the court is exercising its powers in relation to costs. Further, it should be noted that where a party fails to serve a witness statement as required by rules of court, the evidence of the relevant witness is only admissible with the leave of the court. Thus, whilst failure to serve a hearsay notice does not affect the admissibility of hearsay evidence, failure to serve a witness statement in respect of the evidence of a witness which is to be used to prove a hearsay statement may render that evidence inadmissible.

[***Note:*** rules of court (RSC, Ord. 38, r.2A and CCR, Ord. 20, r.15(1)), require parties to civil proceedings to serve witness statements on the other parties. These are written statements of the evidence to be given by their non-expert witnesses. The trial judge may (other than in the case of jury trial) direct that witness statements be treated as the evidence in chief of the relevant witnesses, though cross-examination and re-examination will still take place.]

Calling the maker of a hearsay statement for cross-examination upon it

The effect of Section 3 of the Civil Evidence Act 1995 in conjunction with RSC, Ord. 38, r.22 and CCR, Ord. 20, r.16 (both made under section 3) is that where a party to civil proceedings intends to adduce a hearsay statement in evidence instead of calling its maker as a witness, another party may, within 28 days of the service of the hearsay notice upon him, seek the leave of the court to call the maker and cross-examine him on the hearsay statement as though he had been called by the party who adduced it in evidence.

The evidential weight of a hearsay statement

Essentially, section 4 of the Civil Evidence Act 1995 provides that the court, when considering the evidential weight of a hearsay statement, may take into account any circumstances from which it is reasonable to draw an inference as to its reliability. In particular, section 4 provides that the court may, for this purpose, consider:

- "whether it would have been reasonable and practicable for the party by whom the evidence was adduced to have produced the maker of the original statement as a witness";
- "whether the original statement was made contemporaneously with the occurrence or existence of the matters stated";
- "whether the evidence involves multiple hearsay";
- "whether any person involved had any motive to conceal or misrepresent matters";
- "whether the original statement was an edited account, or was made in collaboration with another or for a particular purpose";
- "whether the circumstances in which the evidence is adduced as hearsay are such as to suggest an attempt to prevent proper evaluation of its weight."

Competence and compellability

Section 5(1) of the Civil Evidence Act 1995 provides that a hearsay statement is inadmissible if its maker would not have been a competent witness at the time of its making. The section also provides that a hearsay statement is inadmissible if proved by a statement made by a person who was not a competent witness at the time when he made his statement.

[*Note:* the competence of witnesses in civil proceedings was considered in Chapter 2 above.]

Credibility

Section 5(2) of the Civil Evidence Act 1995 provides that, where the maker of a hearsay statement is not called as a witness, evidence is admissible to attack or support his credibility to the extent to which it would have been admissible had he been called and evidence of other inconsistent statements which he has made is admissible to contradict the hearsay evidence. The section makes identical provision concerning the credibility and inconsistent statements of the maker of a statement used to prove a hearsay statement. In either case, however, subject to the exceptions identified in Chapter 4 above, the section effectively upholds the principle that evidence cannot be called in rebuttal of answers to collateral questions by providing that evidence relating to a matter cannot be adduced if it could not have been adduced that the maker of the relevant statement been called as a witness and had denied the matter when cross-examined.

Common law exceptions to the hearsay rule

Section 7(1) of the Civil Evidence Act 1995 abolishes what was formally the most important remaining common law exception to the hearsay rule, namely, the rule that informal admissions (namely, statements adverse to their maker's interests) made by a party were admissible in evidence against him. Informal admissions are not admissible under section 1 of the 1995 Act and are thus subject to the provisions of sections 2 to 6 of the Act.

Section 7(2) preserves a number of minor common law exceptions to the hearsay rule (for example, the rule that published works (such as dictionaries) concerning public matters are admissible in evidence. Where evidence is admissible under a preserved common law exception to the hearsay rule, the provisions of sections 2 to 6 of the 1995 Act do not apply to it.

Finally, section 7(3) partially preserves a number of common law rules concerning the admissibility of evidence of reputation, though such evidence must now satisfy the requirements of sections 2 to 6 of the 1995 Act.

Proving statements contained in documents

Section 8 of the Civil Evidence Act 1995 provides that, provided that they are admissible in evidence, statements contained in documents may be proved in civil proceedings either by producing the original documents or by producing copies of the documents or of the relevant parts thereof, authenticated in a manner approved by the court. The section also provides that, for this purpose, a copy need not be directly copied from the original document but may be a copy of a copy, it being irrelevant how may levels of copying there are between the original document and the copy.

[*Note:* production essentially appears to entail calling a witness to produce a document, though it appears that a document may, alternatively, be proved by other admissible evidence (*Ventouris v. Mountain* [1992]). Where a witness is called solely for the purpose of producing a document, the witness need not take the oath (*Perry v. Gibson* (1834).]

Essentially, section 9 provides that it is unnecessary to call witnesses or to adduce other evidence to prove documents which are certified to form part of business or public authority records by officers of the relevant businesses or public authorities. The court may, however, in appropriate circumstances, direct that the provisions of section 9 do not apply to particular documents or types of document.

10. CONFESSIONS

In this Chapter, we will consider both what constitutes a confession and how the courts determine whether confessions are admissible in evidence.

THE MEANING OF "CONFESSION"

Section 82(1) of the Police and Criminal Evidence Act 1984 (PACE) defines a confession as including,

> ". . . any statement wholly or partly adverse to the person who made it, whether made to a person in authority or not and whether made in words or otherwise . . ."

Thus, a statement is a confession if, whether oral, written or made by conduct (*e.g.* by video re-enactment), it is, at least in part, adverse to its maker's interests.

For example, if D, being charged with the murder of V by shooting her, admits that he was the only person who was with V at the time of her death but denies shooting her, V's statement is a confession even though it is partly in his favour because, by placing him at the scene of the crime at the time of its commission, it is, in part, adverse to his interests.

DETERMINING THE ADMISSIBILITY OF A CONFESSION: THE *VOIR DIRE*

The statutory provision which regulates the admissibility of confessions is section 76 of PACE (see below). Challenges to the admissibility of confessions are determined "on the *voir dire*" (*i.e.* in a trial within a trial) during which the jury is not present and the judge is not concerned with the truthfulness of the confession. If the confession is not admitted, then the jury are not told of its existence. If the confession is admitted, it is put before the jury but the defence may still try to persuade the jury that it should not be believed (as the jury are concerned with its truthfulness). If the defence do not challenge the admissibility of a confession before it is put before the jury, it appears that its admissibility cannot subsequently be challenged under section 76 (*R. v. Sat-Bhambra* (1988)), though the defence may still try to persuade the jury that the confession should not be believed. Moreover, if the defence assert that no confession was ever made there is no need for a *voir dire* as it is for the jury, not the judge, to decide whether this is so (*Ajhoda v. The State* (1982)).

Where a *voir dire* is held, the Privy Council stated, in *Wong Kam Ming v. R.* (1980)), that: the accused cannot be questioned about the truthfulness of his confession during the *voir dire*; statements which he makes during the *voir dire* cannot be made known to the jury; and inconsistencies between the accused's evidence and statements which he made during the *voir dire* cannot be made known to the jury unless his confession is admitted.

Finally, if the admissibility of a confession is challenged under section 76 during summary trial, the magistrates must, similarly, hold a trial within a trial (*R. v. Liverpool Juvenile Court* (1988)). During the *voir dire* the magistrates, like the judge in a jury trial, are not concerned with the truthfulness of the confession.

DETERMINING THE ADMISSIBILITY OF A CONFESSION: THE STATUTORY CONDITIONS OF ADMISSIBILITY

If a confession is made by the defendant other than whilst he is testifying in court at his trial, the confession will be hearsay if admitted to prove the truth of its factual content. Confessions are, however, admissible under statute as an exception to the hearsay rule.

The statutory provision which lays down the conditions of admissibility of confessions is section 76 of PACE. Section 76(1) provides for the admissibility of relevant confessions in the criminal trials of their makers, as evidence against their makers, subject to conditions of admissibility laid down by section 76(2). Section 76(1) and (2) provide as follows:

"(1) In any [criminal] proceedings a confession made by an accused person may be given in evidence against him in so far as it is relevant to any matter in issue in the proceedings and is not excluded by the court in pursuance of this section.

(2) If, in any proceedings where the prosecution proposes to give in evidence a confession made by an accused person, it is represented to the court that the confession was or may have been obtained—

    (a) by oppression of the person who made it; or

    (b) in consequence of anything said or done which was likely, in the circumstances existing at the time, to render unreliable any confession which might be made by him in consequence thereof,

    the court shall not allow the confession to be given in evidence against him except in so far as the prosecution proves to the court beyond reasonable doubt that the confession (notwithstanding that it may be true) was not obtained as aforesaid."

Thus, if the defence suggest (or the court of its own motion raises the issue—section 76(3)) that the means by which, or circumstances in which, a confession was obtained fall within paragraphs (a) or (b) of section 76(2), the confession will only be admissible if the prosecution can prove beyond a reasonable doubt that the confession was not obtained in either of the ways set out in those paragraphs. Further, section 76(2) makes clear, and the court has confirmed this in *Crampton* (1991), that whether the confession is true or not is not a relevant consideration in assessing its admissibility.

[***Note:*** students will inevitably be required to demonstrate a high degree of familiarity with section 76(2) in answering examination questions on confessions. Problem questions on confessions will invariably contain examples of conduct, usually on the part of police officers, which may amount to oppression or give rise to unreliability. It is, therefore, extremely important both to know what is meant by oppression and unreliability and to appreciate when oppression and unreliability may render a confession inadmissible.]

Oppression (section 76(2)(a))

In order to establish that a confession was not "obtained by oppression", the prosecution must prove, to the criminal standard of proof, **either** that the accused did not confess in consequence of the oppression to which he was subjected **or** that he was not subjected to oppression.

When is a confession "obtained" by oppression? It appears from the wording of section 76(2)(a) that if the prosecution can prove that the accused did not confess because he was oppressed but for some other reason, then the confession is not rendered inadmissible by paragraph (a). In determining whether the oppression to which the accused was subjected may have "produced" the accused's confession, it seems that the court will take relevant aspects of his personality into account, whether these render it more or less likely that he will "crack" under pressure. Thus, the courts have recognised that conduct which might "persuade" a person of very low intelligence to confess might not have this effect when directed at someone who is intelligent and sophisticated (see, respectively, *R. v. Miller, R. v. Parris, R. v. Abdullahi* (1992) and *R. v. Seelig* (1992)).

The nature of oppression A confession is not rendered inadmissible by section 76(2) if the prosecution can prove that the conduct to which the accused was subjected did not amount to oppression. Section 76(8) provides that oppression includes:

> ". . . torture, inhuman or degrading treatment, and the use or threat of violence (whether or not amounting to torture)."

A more comprehensive definition was adopted in *R. v. Fulling* (1987) by Lord Lane C.J. who stated that oppression should be given its dictionary meaning which, according to the Oxford English Dictionary, is the;

> "Exercise of authority or power in a burdensome, harsh or wrongful manner; unjust or cruel treatment of subjects, inferiors etc; the imposition of unreasonable or unjust burdens."

His Lordship was of the view that oppression in this sense would almost certainly involve improper conduct by persons interviewing the accused.

Examples of conduct on the part of police officers which appears potentially capable of giving rise to oppression include breaches of requirements of PACE or of the Codes of Practice made under PACE and "heavy handed" questioning or distortion of evidence on the part of interviewing officers. For example, it appears that failure to provide access to a solicitor as required by section 58 of PACE may, if a consequence of bad faith, amount to oppression (*R. v. Alladice* (1988)). Similarly, where interviewing officers persistently shouted allegations at the accused even though he had consistently denied his guilt several hundred times over a number of days, their conduct was held to amount to oppression (*R. v. Miller, R. v. Parris, R. v. Abdullahi* (1992)). Again, where interviewing officers deliberately set out to persuade the accused that the case against him is stronger than, in fact, it is, it appears that their conduct may amount to oppression (see *R. v. Beales* (1991)).

Conversely, the mere fact that conduct is improper does not, in itself, mean that the conduct is oppressive if the degree of impropriety is trivial (see *R. v. Emmerson* (1990) and *R. v. Parker* (1995)).

Unreliability (section 76(2)(b))

In order to establish that a confession was not "obtained in consequence of anything said or done which was likely, in the circumstances existing at the time, to render unreliable any confession which [the accused] might [have made] in consequence [of the thing said or done]", the prosecution must prove, to the criminal standard of proof, **either** that the accused did not confess in consequence of the thing said or done, **or** that the thing said or done was not likely to have rendered unreliable any confession made by him in consequence of the thing said or done, in the circumstances in which he did confess.

When is a confession "obtained" in consequence of the thing said or done? It appears from the wording of section 76(2)(b) that if the prosecution can prove that the accused did not confess because the thing was said or done but for some other reason, then the confession is not rendered inadmissible by paragraph (b). In determining whether the thing said or done may have "produced" the accused's confession, it seems that the court will take relevant aspects of his personality into account. Such factors may sometimes make it more likely that the accused confessed in response to the thing said or done but sometimes may have the opposite effect. For example, failure to provide access to a solicitor as required by section 58 of PACE might be a factor which could lead a person of low intelligence who knows little about the criminal process to confess, but may well be less likely to have this effect upon a person who has the ability to cope with an "interview situation" and is aware of his legal rights (see, respectively, *R. v. Harvey* (1988) and *R. v. Alladice* (1988)).

What types of "things" and "circumstances" are capable of producing unreliability? A confession is not rendered inadmissible by section 76(2)(b) if the prosecution can prove that the thing said or done was not likely to have rendered unreliable any confession made by the accused in consequence of the thing said or done in the circumstances in which he did confess.

There is no statutory or common law definition of "unreliable". It appears, however, that, in contrast with oppression, improper conduct does not form an essential pre-requisite of unreliability (*R. v. Fulling*). Further, whether or not the accused's confession is or is not likely to be unreliable is not the issue before the court, the court being concerned with the likely reliability of **any** confession which he might have made in the circumstances, in consequence of the thing said or done (*R. v. Crampton* (1991)).

The court, when deciding whether to exclude a confession under section 76(2)(b), must consider three issues:

(1) whether anything relevant to the operation of paragraph (a) was said or done;

(2) the nature of the circumstances existing at the time when the thing was said or done;

(3) whether in those circumstances, the thing said or done was likely to render any confession which the accused might have made in consequence of the thing said or done unreliable.

Examples of things said or done which might, in appropriate circumstances, be relevant to the operation of paragraph (a) are: breaches of requirements laid down by PACE or by the Codes of Practice made under PACE (*R. v. Trussler* (1988)); inducements to confess in the form of offers of favourable treatment (*R. v. Mathias* (1989)); or statements to the effect that close friends or relatives of the accused are implicated in the commission of the crime under investigation (*R. v. Harvey* (1988)).

The thing said or done must be said or done by someone other than the accused himself (*R. v. Goldenberg* (1988)). Thus, if the accused confesses in the hope that he will be released on bail and, consequently, will be able to obtain alcohol or drugs in order to satisfy his craving, this will not be sufficient to render his confession inadmissible under paragraph (b) unless this hope has been created or fostered by the words or conduct of others.

The circumstances existing at the time when the "thing" was said or done may make it more or less likely that a consequent confession would be unreliable. For example, the absence of a legal adviser may result in the accused attaching more weight to an inducement to confess than he would have done had he received proper legal advice before confessing (*R. v. Mathias* (1989)). Similarly, the mental illness and low intelligence of the accused may increase the likelihood that, upon hearing that her lover has confessed to a crime, she would confess in order to protect her (*R. v. Harvey* (1988)).

Finally, the fact that circumstances which make it more likely that a confession made by the accused will be unreliable are unknown to the interviewing officers at the time when they say or do the relevant thing does not prevent the court from taking account of those circumstances when determining the admissibility of the accused's confession under paragraph (b). Thus, for example, the fact that the officers are not aware of the accused's low mental age would not prevent the court from considering this factor when considering whether things said or done by the officers were likely to have rendered unreliable a consequent confession by him (see *R. v. Everett* (1988)).

Judicial discretion to refuse to permit the prosecution to adduce a confession in evidence

[***Note:*** in answering exam questions on confessions, students will normally be required not only to consider whether a confession is rendered inadmissible by section 76(2) but will also be required to consider whether, upon the assumption that the operation of section 76(2) does not render the confession inadmissible, the court should exclude the confession in the exercise of its exclusionary discretion.]

Where the operation of section 76(2) of PACE does not render a confession inadmissible as prosecution evidence, the court (trial judge or magistrates) may permit the prosecution to adduce the confession in evidence, but is not obliged to do so. Rather, the court possesses discretion to refuse to permit the prosecution to adduce a confession in evidence.

The basis of this exclusionary discretion (which extends to all forms of prosecution evidence, not just to confessions) is section 78 of PACE, which provides that the court may refuse to allow the prosecution to adduce evidence,

> "... if it appears to the court that having regard to all the circumstances, including the circumstances in which the evidence was obtained, the admission of the evidence would have such an adverse effect on the fairness of the proceedings that the court ought not to admit it."

Whilst, in practice, the courts usually make use of section 78 when refusing to admit confession evidence in the exercise of their discretion, the extent of their discretion is not limited to circumstances encompassed by section 78. Rather, section 82(3) preserves the discretion to exclude prosecution evidence which the criminal courts possessed prior to the enactment of PACE.

Essentially, the effect of these two provisions of PACE, when viewed together, appears to be that the criminal courts are prepared to exclude confessions in the exercise of their discretion for the following reasons, though it is not suggested that this list is exhaustive.

(a) *Where there has been a breach of requirement laid down either by PACE or by one of the Codes of Practice made under PACE:* It appears that the exercise of exclusionary discretion is justified where the breach is "significant and substantial", though the fact that a breach is significant and substantial does not automatically require the exclusion of a confession in every case (*R. v. Walsh* (1989).

Thus, it may not be appropriate to exclude a confession in respect of a breach which is trivial (such as not showing the accused the record of his interview—*R. v. Matthews* (1989)) or which has insignificant practical consequences. For example, the court may decline to exercise its discretion where, although there has been a failure to provide the accused with a solicitor as requested, the court is satisfied that this has not adversely affected the accused's interests because he has the ability to cope with an "interview situation" and is aware of his legal rights (*R. v. Alladice* (1988)).

In contrast, if a breach has significant practical consequences, the exercise of exclusionary discretion may well be appropriate. Thus, if the court is of the opinion that the accused would probably not have confessed had he received legal advice as requested, the court is likely to exercise its exclusionary discretion (*R. v. Samuel* (1988)).

Further, even where a breach does not have significant practical consequences, bad faith on the part of the interviewer may persuade the court to exercise its discretion. Thus, where the court is satisfied that failure to provide the accused with a solicitor did not adversely affect his interests, the court may still be prepared to exercise its exclusionary discretion if the failure to comply with the accused's request amounted to a deliberate decision not to comply with the requirements of PACE (*R. v. Alladice* (1988)).

(b) *Where a confession has been obtained by unfair means:* In *R. v. Mason* (1987) police officers told the accused and his solicitor that the accused's fingerprints had been found at the scene of the crime (arson) on a bottle containing inflammable liquid. This was a deliberate lie but it persuaded the accused's solicitor to advise him to answer police questions and explain his involvement in the offence with the result that he confessed. The Court of Appeal held that the trial judge should have excluded the confession in the exercise of his discretion.

(c) *Where the probative value of the confession is outweighed by its prejudicial effect:* As has already been seen, judicial discretion is commonly exercised for this reason where the court excludes evidence of the accused's previous convictions (see Chapter 12 below). If, however, the judge feels that the evidential value of a confession is small (perhaps, for example, because of the mental illness of the accused at the time when he made it, he may be prepared to exercise his exclusionary discretion so as to prevent the jury being prejudiced by knowledge of the confession (*R. v. Miller* (1986)).

What if a first confession is excluded but the accused has confessed at a later interview which was properly conducted? Sometimes, following the making of a confession which the court either cannot admit, due to the operation of section 76(2), or will not admit in the exercise of its discretion, it may be that the accused was interviewed again, and made a further confession. Where this is the case, even if nothing happened in the course of the second interview which would require or justify exclusion of the confession, the courts have held that the conduct which required or justified exclusion of the first confession may remain an operative factor which either requires the exclusion of the second on grounds of oppression or unreliability or justifies its exclusion in the exercise of judicial discretion (see, respectively, *R. v. Ismail* (1991); *R. v. McGovern* (1991); and *R. v. Gillard and Barrett* (1991)).

Is an accused's confession admissible evidence for the prosecution against his co-accused? Usually, a confession is only admissible in evidence for the prosecution against the person who made it. It cannot be used against a co-accused whom it implicates as this would infringe the hearsay rule, the hearsay exception contained in section 76 of PACE only permitting the admission of a confession as evidence against its maker. There are, however, two exceptional situations in which a confession made by one person can be used as evidence against another.

First, if an accused, whilst being interviewed, accepts that a confession, implicating him, which was made by a co-accused is true, the confession also becomes his confession and may be used against him.

Secondly, for limited purposes, a confession made by one conspirator may be used as evidence against another in a conspiracy trial.

Is an accused's confession admissible in evidence for a co-accused?

In *R. v. Myers* (1997), the House of Lords held that in so far as an accused's confession is relevant to establish the defence of a co-accused or to undermine the prosecution's case against the co-accused, the co-accused may adduce the confession in evidence as evidence of the facts stated provided the confession was not obtained in such a manner as would have led to its exclusion under section 76 of PACE 1984.

Admissibility of facts discovered as a result of a confession

Sometimes when an accused makes a confession, he also provides information as to the where-abouts of items connected with the offence (*e.g.* the murder weapon) which the prosecution may later wish to adduce in evidence against him. The admissibility and evidential significance of such evidence depends, to some extent, upon the admissibility of the confession itself.

(a) *Where the confession is admissible:* Evidence of the discovery of relevant items in consequence of the confession is also admissible, the prosecution being entitled to reveal to the jury how the items were discovered.

(b) *Where the confession is excluded under section 76 of PACE:* The effect of section 76(4) is that the fact that the items have been discovered in a particular location is still admissible. The effect of section 76(5) and 76(6) is, however, that the prosecution cannot reveal to the jury how the items were discovered.

For example, assume that D confesses to burglary. As a result, stolen property is found in his car. The confession is excluded under section 76. The fact that the property was found in his car is admissible but the prosecution may not refer to the confession. Thus, they cannot reveal to the jury that the police searched D's car because D had told them when he confessed that the stolen property could be found there.

In this example, the fact that the property was found in D's car in cogent evidence against him even though the confession is inadmissible. Suppose, however, that D had informed the police that he had stolen the property and left it in a stolen car. In this case, if D's confession was inadmissible and the stolen car could not be linked to D in some other way, th fact that the property was discovered in the stolen car would appear to be of limited evidential significance.

(c) *Where the confession is excluded in the exercise of the common law or statutory discretion:* Section 76(4) provides that it only applies where a confession is "excluded in pursuance of" section 76. It does not apply where, in the exercise of its discretion, the court refuses to allow the prosecution to adduce a confession in evidence. It appears, however, that in such circumstances, common law principles, the effect of which is similar to that of section 76(4), will probably apply (*R. v. Warickshall* (1783) provides an example of the application of these common law principles prior to the enactment of PACE).

Like section 76(4), sections 76(5) and (6) only apply where a confession is "excluded in pursuance of" section 76. The common law position concerning the extent to which the prosecution may reveal to the jury how the items were discovered where the court excludes a confession in the exercise of its discretion is unclear.

Excluded confessions as evidence of their makers' manner of communication Section 76(4) also provides that:

"The fact that a confession is wholly or partly excluded in pursuance of this section shall not affect the admissibility in evidence—

(b) where the confession is relevant as showing that the accused speaks, writes or expresses himself in a particular way, of so much of the confession as is necessary to show that he does so."

When a confession is excluded under section 76 part or all of it may still be admissible to prove that its maker "speaks, writes or expresses himself in a particular way", where this is relevant to an issue before the court (PACE section 76(4)(b)). Only so much of the confession as is required to prove the accused's manner of communication is admissible.

Confessions made by unaccompanied mentally handicapped persons Where a confession made by a mentally handicapped person in the absence of an independent person is admitted in evidence against him and the prosecution case is based wholly or substantially upon the confession, section 77 of PACE applies. The effect of section 77 is, essentially, that the trial judge must explain to the jury (or that the magistrates must be aware) that, in the circumstances, they must exercise especial caution prior to convicting the accused.

This requirement does not apply if an independent person (*i.e.* a person independent of the police force) was present when the accused confessed.

[**Note:** in many cases in which a mentally handicapped person confesses in the absence of an independent person section 77 will be irrelevant in practice as the confession will be excluded under section 76 or in the exercise of judicial discretion. The provision of a warning under section 77 does not render admissible a confession which otherwise would be excluded (*R. v. Moss* (1990).]

11. STATUTORY EXCEPTIONS TO THE HEARSAY RULE IN CRIMINAL PROCEEDINGS (OTHER THAN CONFESSIONS)

This Chapter deals with the statutory exceptions to the hearsay rule (other than confessions) which permit the admission of **documentary hearsay only.** There are statutory exceptions other than those examined in this chapter. However, only those exceptions which feature most commonly in examination questions are considered here, *i.e.* section 23 and section 24 of the Criminal Justice Act 1988 and section 69 of the Police and Criminal Evidence Act 1984 (PACE). These provisions are exceptions to the hearsay rule only. Consequently, they do not render admissible statements which are inadmissible because they fall within another exclusionary rule of evidence in addition to the hearsay rule.

SECTIONS 23 & 24

Before considering the individual requirements which must be satisfied in order to admit a statement under either of these sections, it is appropriate to note certain points applicable to both sections.

Points to note:

(1) Only a hearsay "statement ... in a document" may be admitted under either section. A statement is "any representation of fact" and a document is anything in which information of any description is recorded" (see schedule 1, paragraph 12 of the Civil Evidence Act 1995).

(2) Neither section will render admissible a confession which would not be admissible under section 76 of PACE.

(3) Both sections are subject to section 69 of PACE which
    applies to documents produced by computers. As a con-
    sequence, a hearsay statement which was produced by a
    computer must, in addition to satisfying the requirements
    of either section 23 or section 24, also satisfy the require-
    ments of section 69 if it is to be admissible in evidence.

Section 23

Requirements for admission under section 23

(1) A hearsay statement will only be admissible under section
    23 if the maker of the statement could have given direct
    oral evidence of the relevant facts.

   If the maker could not have given direct oral testimony
   of the facts because his oral evidence would itself have been
   hearsay, the statement will be inadmissible under section
   23 (see *Re Koscot Interplanetary UK Ltd* (1972) (a Civil Evidence Act 1968 case)).

(2) *The statement was made in the document.* Only a documentary
    hearsay statement which was actually made in the docu-
    ment may be adduced under section 23. The same term was
    used in the Civil Evidence Act 1968 and the criminal courts
    have adopted a definition of the term in line with that
    formerly applied in civil proceedings under the 1968
    Act.

   The leading case in criminal proceedings is *R. v. McGillivray* (1992). The maker of a statement was severely injured
   and made his statement to a policeman from his hospital
   bed, in the presence of his nurse. His statement was then
   read back to him and, although his injuries meant that he
   was unable to sign it, he acknowledged its accuracy. The
   court held that he had made his statement in a document
   because a person makes a statement in a document if he:
   (a) writes it down; OR (b) dictates it to someone else who
   writes it down and then checks it over and signs or otherwise
   approves it.

   A third situation in which a person makes a statement in
   a document derives from *Ventouris v. Mountain* (No. 2)
   (1992). The case was decided under the Civil Evidence Act
   1968, but the definition is equally applicable in criminal proceedings. This case provides that a person makes a state-

ment in a document if, intending to be taped and with his knowledge, he is tape recorded making the statement.
(3) One of the statutory reasons contained in section 23 for not calling the maker of the statement must be satisfied.

Where the prosecution seek to rely on a statutory reason, they must prove the reason exists beyond a reasonable doubt (see *R. v. Minors* (1989)) but where the defence wish to rely on a statutory reason, the requisite standard of proof is on a balance of probabilities (see *R. v. Mattey and Queeley* (1995)).

What are the statutory reasons? The statutory reasons for not calling the maker of the statement are that he:

(i) is **dead** OR
(ii) is **unfit to attend as a witness by reason of his bodily or mental condition** OR
(iii) is **outside the United Kingdom and it is not reasonably practicable to secure his attendance** OR
(iv) **cannot be found, all reasonable steps having been taken to find him** OR
(v) **does not give oral evidence through fear or because he is kept out of the way, the statement having been made to a police officer or some other person charged with the duty of investigating offenders.**

Points to note about the courts' interpretation of the statutory reasons in section 23:

(1) "Unfit to attend as a witness . . ." applies not only to a witness's physical inability to testify but also his mental capacity to testify and, therefore, includes a witness's inability to recall facts in a coherent manner (see *R. v. Setz-Dempsey Richardson* (1994)).
(2) The reason that the witness "is outside the UK . . ." cannot be used in respect of a witness who resides in a foreign embassy within the United Kingdom (see *Carmenza Jiminez-Paez* (1994)).
(3) With regard to the practicability of securing the attendance of a witness who is outside the United Kingdom, this should be determined at the date of the application to admit the witness's statement (see *R. v. French and Gowhar* (1993)), and by taking into account: (i) the importance of the witness's evidence and whether or not it is prejudicial; (ii) the issues of cost and inconvenience and

(iii) the arguments raised as to why attendance is not reasonably practicable (see *R. v. Castillo* (1996)).

(4) The reason that the witness "does not give oral evidence through fear ..." has caused problems of interpretation in that it is not clear whether the witness's "fear" must be fear for his own personal safety or whether it can be given a broad definition to include fear for the safety of others and fear of prosecution or of publicity. What is clear, however, is that the fear need not be related to the offence in question (*R. v. Martin* (1996)) or be based on reasonable grounds provided it is a "consequence of the commission of the material offence or of something said or done subsequently in relation to that offence and the possibility of the witness testifying as to it" (see *R. v. Acton Justices, ex parte McMullen* (1990)). Also, only evidence which is itself admissible may be used to prove the witness's fear (see *Neill v. North Antrim Magistrates Court* (1992)).

Section 24

Requirements for admission under section 24

(1) The statement must actually be in a document.
    Thus, statements which were made in a document and those which were not but which are located in a document may be admitted under section 24.
(2) The document was created or received by a person in the course of a trade, business, profession or other occupation, or as the holder of a paid or unpaid office.
    Who must act in the course of a trade, business profession, etc? No obligation is imposed on the supplier of the information to have acted in the course of his trade, business or profession. Only the person who created or received the document must have done so in such capacity. Where, however, the information contained in the document passes through intermediaries before reaching the person who creates or receives the document, the intermediaries must also receive the information in the course of a trade, business, profession, etc.
(3) The information contained in the document was supplied by a person who had, or may reasonably be supposed to have had, personal knowledge of the matters dealt with.
(4) A fourth requirement is imposted if the statement was prepared for the purposes of pending or contemplated criminal

proceedings or for the purposes of a criminal investigation. Section 24(4) provides that a documentary statement prepared for any of the aforementioned reasons will not be admissible under section 24 unless:

(a) there is a section 23 statutory reason for not calling the person who made the statement (see section 24(4)(b)(i) & (ii)) OR

(b) the reason the maker is not called is that he cannot reasonably be expected (having regard to the time which has elapsed since he made the statement and to all the circumstances) to have any recollection of the matters dealt with in his statement (see section 24(4)(b)(iii)).

This fourth requirement raises several important practical questions:

In order to admit a statement under section 24 is it always necessary to establish a section 23 reason or show that the maker cannot reasonably be expected to have any recollection of the matters dealt with in his statement? The answer to this is clearly no. It is only necessary to establish one of the aforementioned reasons if the statement was prepared for the purposes of pending or contemplated criminal proceedings or for the purposes of a criminal investigation. For example, if an attempt is made to adduce under section 24 the written statement of a witness to a criminal offence who made his statement to a policeman investigating the offence or to a solicitor who represents the accused, the fourth requirement will apply. However, if a statement was made before a criminal investigation is underway or before criminal proceedings are contemplated, only the first three requirements set out above must be satisfied in order to admit the statement under section 24.

Who is the maker for the purposes of section 24(4)? For the purposes of section 23, there is no argument that the maker of the statement is the person who makes it in the first place, *i.e.* the initial supplier of the information. However, this person may not be treated as being the maker for the purposes of section 24(4). The possible difference in interpretation of the term arises because of the precise wording of section 24(1)(ii). This subsection refers to the information contained in the document being "supplied by a person (whether or not the maker of the statement) . . ." and, thus, clearly envisages the possibility of the supplier and the maker being two different people. Consequently, when the criminal courts were required to consider whether the maker was the actual supplier of the information or the person who took down what the supplier said to him, it was held that the maker was in fact the latter, see *Brown v. Secretary of State for Social Security* (1994). An obvious criticism of such an interpretation is, however, that it requires a reason for not calling someone who may not have been able to give oral evidence on the matter anyway because his evidence would have been inadmissible as hearsay. An example illustrates the point.

Example: A witnesses B murder C. The police are unable to find any suspects and eventually A, not wishing to get involved, makes an anonymous phone call to the police some time later, naming B as the murderer and explaining what she had seen. Y, a policeman, writes down everything A tells him but A hangs up before Y has a chance to read back to her what he has written. B is charged with murder but A has still not been located by the time of the trial. Y, however, is available to testify. The prosecution with to adduce the statement taken down by Y of his telephone conversation with A. The statement cannot be adduced under section 23 because A, the maker for the purposes of section 23, did not make her statement in the document. Nor can it be admitted under section 24 because it was prepared for the purposes of a criminal investigation and, if *Brown* is followed, it is Y who will be treated as the maker and there is no statutory reason for not calling him (and even though his oral evidence would have been inadmissible as hearsay anyway). The issue of the identity of the maker for the purposes of section 24 does not appear to be settled though, in light of the decision of the Court of Appeal in *R. v. Lockley* (1995). The Court did not refer to *Brown* in *Lockley* and treated the maker as being the supplier of the information.

If relying on the reason contained in section 24(4)(b)(iii), must it be proved that the maker cannot reasonably be expected to remember the whole of his statement? This question was considered in *R. v. Carrington* (1994) in which the court held that the section 24(4)(b)(iii) reason can still be relied upon where the witness cannot recollect a part of a statement but can recollect the rest of it on the basis that a document can be treated as made up of several independent statements, some of which a witness may remember and some of which he may not. Thus, on the facts, a part of an exhibit which contained details of a car registration number was treated as a separate statement from the rest of the exhibit and the prosecution could rely on the reason that the maker could not remember details of the registration number for the purposes of section 24(4)(b)(iii) even though she could recall the contents of other parts of the document.

SECTION 69 OF PACE

As explained earlier in this chapter, a party wishing to adduce a hearsay statement produced by a computer as proof of its contents must satisfy section 69 of PACE in addition to section 23 or section 24. However, section 69 is not restricted in its application to hearsay statements—it must be satisfied in order to adduce any kind of statement produced by a computer as proof of its contents, be the statement hearsay or not, see *R. v. Shephard* (1993). Section 69 will not apply though, if the printout itself is not adduced in evidence (see *R. v. Golizadeh* (1995)).

What is the purpose of section 69?

The aim of section 69 is to ensure that statements produced by a computer are not admitted unless there is evidence that the computer has correctly stored, processed and reproduced the information provided. It is not the aim of the section to require the prosecution to prove that the statement is true (see *DPP v. McKeown* (1997)).

What is the definition of "computer"? There is no definition of computer in the statute. In *Shephard*, the court held that the word should be given its ordinary meaning. It is unclear whether the ordinary meaning of "computer" is wide enough to encompass a word processor although the court in *R. v. Blackburn* (1993) doubted, obiter, that it would be.

Requirements for admission under section 69

The following requirements must be satisfied:

(a) There are no reasonable grounds for believing that the statement is inaccurate because of improper use of the computer.
(b) At all material times the computer was operating properly, or if not, any respect in which it was not operating properly or was out of operation was not such as to affect the production of the document or the accuracy of its contents.
(c) Any relevant condition specified by rules of court is satisfied.

A written certificate purporting to be signed by a person occupying a responsible position in relation to the operation of the com-

puter is normally sufficient proof that the aforementioned conditions have been met, although the court has the power to require
oral testimony to this effect.

THE COURT'S POWER TO REFUSE TO ADMIT STATEMENTS WHICH ARE ADMISSIBLE UNDER SECTION 23 OR SECTION 24

Section 25

What is the purpose of section 25? Section 25 provides the
court with a discretion to exclude statements admissible under section 23 or section 24. The court's common law exclusionary discretion and its discretion under section 78 of PACE (both of which
apply to prosecution evidence only) may be used to exclude statements which the prosecution seek to adduce under section 23 or
section 24. However, in practice, section 25, which specifically
applies to hearsay statements to be adduced under section 23 or
section 24, but which is wider in scope in that it applies to statements adduced by either the prosecution or the defence, is more
commonly relied upon.

What is the basis for exclusion under section 25? The court
may exercise its discretion under section 25 if of the opinion that,
in the circumstances, the statement ought not to be admitted in
the interests of justice.

Section 26

In addition to the power to exclude statements in the exercise of
its discretion, the court also has the power under section 26 to
refuse leave to admit a statement even though the requirements
of section 23 or section 24 are satisfied.

When is leave required under section 26? Section 26 provides
that leave is required to adduce a statement which is admissible
under section 23 or section 24 if it was prepared for the purposes
of pending or contemplated criminal proceedings or of a criminal
investigation.

What is the basis for granting leave under section 26? The
basis for granting leave under section 26 is the same as that for
excluding under section 25, *i.e.* leave shall not be given unless the

court is of the opinion that the statement's admission is in the interests of justice.

The relationship between section 25 and section 26

What is the difference between section 25 and section 26?
The main difference between section 25 and section 26 is that under the former section the party objecting to the admission of the statement must demonstrate that it is not in the interests of justice to admit it whereas under the latter section the party seeking leave to adduce the statement must demonstrate that it is in the interests of justice to admit it (see *R. v. Patel & Others* (1993)).

Which factors will the court take into consideration in determining whether to exercise its discretion under section 25 or to grant leave under section 26?
Section 25 requires the court to have regard to all the circumstances but sets out the following factors as being particularly relevant:

   (i) whether the document is likely to be authentic;
  (ii) whether the statement appears to supply evidence which would not otherwise be readily available;
 (iii) the relevance of the evidence which it does supply to issues which are likely to have to be determined in the proceedings; and
  (iv) the risk that the admission or exclusion of the statement may result in unfairness to the accused (including whether it is likely to be possible to controvert the statement if the person making it does not attend to give oral evidence).

The matters which the court is specifically directed to consider in deciding whether to grant leave under section 26 are not reproduced as they are broadly similar to those which they must consider under section 25. One difference between the two is that section 26 specifically refers to the contents of the statement and section 25 does not. However, as neither list of factors is exhaustive, and the court is required to consider under both sections any factor which is relevant, the contents of the statement is likely to be relevant under section 25 also. Further, the courts' interpretation of a factor under one section will apply equally to that factor when considered under the other section.

The following factors have so far been considered by the courts:

(a) *The contents of the statement.* The quality of the evidence being adduced was described as being a "crucial factor" in *Scott v. The Queen* (1984).

(b) *Whether it is likely to be possible to controvert the statement.* It was stated in *R. v. Cole* (1990) that the weight which should be attached to the fact that the witness cannot be cross-examined and the harm which this could cause to the fairness of the proceedings will vary from case to case and will depend upon the quality of the evidence shown by the contents of the statement.

(c) *Any other circumstances.* In *R. v. French and Gowhar*, the court held that this term could encompass the prosecution's application for severance which had caused a delay in the proceedings and resulted in the unavailability to testify of the witness whose statement it was sought to adduce.

How are section 25 and section 26 applied in practice? It is obvious from what has already been noted that there is a great deal of overlap between section 25 and section 26 and that it is unlikely that in a situation in which both sections are relevant that the court would decide to grant leave under section 26 and then choose to exclude under section 25, the relevant considerations for both decisions being the same. Thus, the court held in *R. v. Grafton* (1995) that where a statement falls under the umbrella of section 26 it will, in most cases, be necessary to consider only whether, taking into account all relevant factors, to grant leave under section 26 without separate consideration of section 25.

The decision in *Grafton* does not mean that, for examination purposes, you should not refer to section 25 if section 26 is relevant. You must refer to both sections but then, having considered any factors relevant to the operation of section 26, proceed to explain that, if the court decides to grant leave, it is unlikely to then go on to consider whether to exclude under section 25.

CREDIBILITY PROOF AND WEIGHT

With regard to statements admitted under section 23 or section 24, evidence relating to the maker's credibility is admissible even though he does not testify (see schedule 2, paragraph 5).

Section 27 provides that a statement contained in a document which is admissible in criminal proceedings may be proved by the production of the document or of a copy thereof authenticated in a manner approved by the court.

In determining the weight of evidence admitted under section 23 or section 24, the court can consider all relevant circumstances from which an inference as to the document's accuracy can be drawn (see schedule 2, paragraph 3).

12. SIMILAR FACT EVIDENCE

In criminal proceedings, evidence of the accused's bad character may, in limited circumstances, be admissible as evidence of his guilt. Such evidence may be admissible for this purpose either under a statutory provision, such as section 27(3) of the Theft Act 1968, or under the common law. Where such evidence is tendered for this purpose under the common law it is commonly referred to as "similar fact evidence". Similar fact evidence may also be admissible in civil proceedings.

[**Note:** it may be that previous convictions are not properly admissible as similar fact evidence (*R. v. Shepherd* (1980)). If this is correct, the relevant bad character of the accused may be proved in a variety of other ways (*e.g.* via his guilty pleas or confessions, during cross-examination of him or examination of other witnesses.]

THE ADMISSIBILITY OF SIMILAR FACTS EVIDENCE FOR THE PROSECUTION IN CRIMINAL PROCEEDINGS

Is similar fact evidence admissible as evidence of the accused's disposition for the purpose of inviting the court to infer that because he has "done it before" he has probably "done it again"?

Similar fact evidence is not admissible merely for this purpose. That this is so was clearly stated by Herschell L.C. in *Makin v. Attorney-General for New South Wales* (1894). Thus, in *Noor Mohamed v. R.* (1949), the Privy Council held that evidence to the effect that the accused's wife had died from cyanide poisoning and that he might have tricked her into taking cyanide which was in his possession for business purposes should not have been admitted to prove that he subsequently poisoned with cyanide the woman with whom he was living, there being no evidence of such a trick in the latter case.

When is similar fact evidence admissible?

Similar fact evidence is admissible when it is relevant to an issue before the court (*Makin v. Attorney-General for New South Wales*) **provided** that in the opinion of the trial judge the probative value of the similar fact evidence justifies its admission in the context of the prejudicial effect which its admission will produce (*DPP v. Boardman* (1975)).

[*Note*: when a trial judge balances the probative value of similar fact evidence against its prejudicial effect in order to determine whether to admit the evidence, it is unclear whether the judge does so in the course of exercising his exclusionary discretion or whether in so doing he is determining a question of fact and degree. Indeed, support for both views may be derived from the decision of the House of Lords in *DPP v. Boardman*. It is submitted that the better view is that the question is one of fact and degree (see *DPP v. P.* (1991) and *R. v. Gurney* (1994)), though there is ample support for the contrary view (see, for example, *R. v. Johnson* (1995) and *R. v. Peters* (1995), the Court of Appeal in both cases treating the balancing process as amounting to an exercise of exclusionary discretion). In practice, however, whichever view as to the nature of the balancing process in correct, the test which the trial judge is required to apply when considering the admissibility of similar fact evidence for the prosecution is effectively the same. Thus, it is submitted that the question is one of technical rather than one of practical significance.]

Relevance: In order to be admissible, similar fact evidence must be relevant to an issue before the court. This was the case in *Makin v. Attorney-General for New South Wales*, in which the trial judge properly admitted evidence to the effect that several dead babies had been found buried in the curtilage of houses which the two co-accused had occupied and that they had "adopted" these babies in return for financial payments which were inadequate to maintain them. The evidence was admitted in the context of a murder trial concerning the death of another baby which the accused had "adopted" in return for a similar payment, the baby being found buried in their garden. The similar fact evidence was admitted to prove that the baby's death had not been accidental.

Equally, in *R. v. Straffen* (1952), similar fact evidence was properly admitted to identify the accused as the murderer of a girl. Several people, including the accused, had passed the place where the girl's body was found during the period in which she was killed. Unlike the others, however, the accused had previously killed two other girls in a similar way and in similar circumstances.

In contrast, the evidence concerning the death of the accused's wife in Noor Mohamed's case does not appear to have been of relevance to an issue before the court. The position might have been different had there been evidence to suggest that the accused had tricked the other woman into taking the poison, but there was no such evidence.

[**Note:** there is no rule to the effect that similar fact evidence is only admissible for the purpose of rebutting a defence which the accused has raised (*Harris v. DPP* (1952)).]

Probative value and prejudicial effect Obviously, where similar fact evidence such as that encountered in *Makin* or *Straffen* is admitted, this is likely to prejudice the jury against the accused. Even where similar fact evidence is relevant to an issue before the court, the judge should only admit the evidence where, in his opinion, the probative value of the evidence justifies its admission in the context of its prejudicial effect (*DPP v. Boardman*).

For example, with reference to the facts of Straffen's case, it must be extremely likely upon such facts that a jury will conclude that a man who has twice killed girls in the past is guilty of a subsequent similar killing. Upon the facts of the case, however, it appears that the similarities between the three killings were such that a properly directed jury would have been entitled to conclude that the same person killed all three girls. Consequently, the accused having admitted the first two killings, the similar fact evidence tended to identify him as the killer of the third girl. Thus, even though the similar fact evidence was extremely prejudicial, it was also strongly probative of the accused's guilt.

Equally, with reference to the facts of Noor Mohamed's case, it must be likely that, where it is suggested to a jury that a man may have tricked his wife into taking cyanide, the jury will conclude that he is responsible for the death of the woman with whom he was living by cyanide poisoning. Upon the facts of the case, however, the accused had neither admitted the murder of his wife nor had he been convicted or even charged with her murder and, moreover, there was no evidence that the second woman had been tricked into taking the poison. Consequently, the similar fact evidence did not tend to prove that the accused had murdered the second woman but it was extremely prejudicial.

Between the facts of cases like *Straffen*, in which very prejudicial evidence possesses great probative value, and those of cases like, *Noor Mohamed*, in which very prejudicial evidence possesses little or no probative value, there exists a virtually limitless spectrum of possible factual variations which a trial judge may encounter when required to determine the admissibility of similar fact evidence. Where similar fact evidence is relevant to an issue before the court, and thus possesses some probative value, the judge must perform the difficult task of balancing its probative value against its prejudicial effect in order to determine whether it should be admitted. In some cases, the prejudicial effect of the similar fact evidence may be limited. This might be the case, for example, where the previous conduct revealed to the jury as similar fact evidence does not, even if true, amount to a criminal offence (see, for example, the facts of *R. v. Butler* (1986)). In other cases, as has already been seen, the prejudicial effect of the evidence may be such that only substantial probative value could justify its admission.

Striking similarity Essentially, striking similarity means a similarity of features other than those which are merely commonplace such that there is no possibility of coincidence. For example, in Straffen's case, both the similar fact evidence and the case before the court concerned the murder of young girls by manual strangulation, all three killings being apparently motiveless with no signs of a struggle, no sexual interference and no attempt to conceal the body. Even though persons other than the accused had passed through the area in which the crime was committed during the period in which it was committed, the likelihood that one of the others was also a child murderer who murdered girls by manual strangulation, without motive, a struggle, sexual interference or an attempt to conceal the boxy was so remote that the possibility that the accused's presence could be regarded as a coincidence could, it is submitted, properly be discounted. Thus, the similarities were clearly striking.

Clearly, striking similarity is a source of high probative value which can justify the admission of similar fact evidence (see *DPP v. Boardman*). It should be noted, however, that, in *DPP v. P.* (1991), the House of Lords made clear that, subject to one exception, striking similarity is not required in order for similar fact evidence to be admissible. Thus, in general, striking similarity forms one possible source of high probative value but is neither the only such source nor does it form an essential pre-requisite of the admission of such evidence.

The one exceptional situation referred to in which it appears that striking similarity will normally be required if similar fact evidence is to be admitted is where, as in Straffen's case, such evidence is used as evidence of identification. That evidence of a "signature" or "special feature" may be required in identification cases was recognised by Mackay L.C. in *DPP v. P.*

[**Note:** whether striking similarity forms an essential pre-requisite to the admissibility of similar fact evidence in identification cases (*R. v. Johnson* (1995)), or, rather, is something which, as a matter of practice, will normally be required in such cases if the requisite probative value is to exist (*R. v. Lee* (1996)) remains open to doubt, though it is submitted that the latter view is to be preferred.]

Probative force without striking similarity In *DPP v. P.*, Mackay L.C. did not attempt to exhaustively define the nature of those circumstances in which sufficiently great probative value to justify the admission of similar fact evidence may arise in the absence of striking similarity. His Lordship did, however, provide some guidance with reference to cases of the type with which the House of Lords was concerned in *DPP v. P.*

DPP v. P. concerned charges of rape and incest by a father in respect of his two daughters. The counts were tried together, the judge refusing to sever the indictment and also admitting the evidence of one daughter upon the trial of the counts concerning the other. No issue of identification arose, the question being, rather, whether the alleged offences had, in fact, been committed.

In the House of Lords, Mackay L.C. indicated that, in such a case, the question for the trial judge to determine is whether the evidence of one daughter provides support for that of the other which is sufficiently strong to make it just to admit it in the context of its prejudicial effect. His Lordship recognised that such support may be derived from striking similarity in the manner in which a crime is committed but also indicated that it may be derived from other relationships in time and in circumstances.

Upon the facts of the case, his Lordship held that the similar fact evidence possessed sufficient probative force to justify its admission in evidence. His Lordship indicated that the source of this probative force was the combination of a number of circumstances. First, both girls described a prolonged course of conduct in relation to each. Secondly, force was used in relation to each. Thirdly, they and their mother were generally dominated and the silence was secured by threats. Fourthly, their father was obsessed with keeping his daughters for himself. Fifthly, when the elder daughter left home the younger daughter adopted her role. Sixthly, there was evidence that the father had paid for his daughters' abortions.

[***Note***: at one time the courts effectively adopted a more generous approach to the admission of similar fact evidence in relation to sexual offence cases (and particularly in cases involving homosexuality or offences against children) than they did in relation to other types of cases (see *Thompson v. R.* (1918) and *R. v. Sims* (1946)). The decisions of the House of Lords in *DPP v. Boardman* (concerning sexual offences by a headmaster against male pupils) and in *DPP v. P.* (concerning sexual offences against children) have, however, clearly established that the principles governing the admissibility of similar facts evidence in sexual offence cases (whether or not involving homosexuality) are the same as those which govern its admission in general.]

An example of the admission of similar fact evidence in the absence of striking similarity subsequent to the decision of the House of Lords in *DPP v. P.* is provided by *R. v. Gurney* (1994)). In Gurney's case the accused's previous conviction for burglary was held by the Court of Appeal to have been properly admitted as evidence of intent, no issue of identification arising. The accused had admitted breaking into a flat but claimed that he did so intending to steal, the prosecution had alleged that he intended to rape. The Court of Appeal regarded the most significant similarities between the facts of the case before it and those of the previous offence as being that in both cases: the female complainants were thought to live by themselves; the accused had a weapon with him (the weapon being of a different type in each case); the accused did not try to escape when discovered by the female complainant; and the accused did not try to steal anything even though he had the opportunity to do so.

In a case like *DPP v. P.*, is similar fact evidence admissible if it is suggested that the complainants have colluded?

In recent years, the significance of alleged collusion between witnesses in the context of the admissibility of similar fact evidence has been unclear. In *R. v. H.* (1995), however, the House of Lords clarified the position. Thus, it is now clear that, in general, the trial judge should ignore the possibility of collusion when determining whether similar fact evidence is admissible. Rather, where an allegation of collusion is made, it will normally be for the jury, properly directed by the judge, to determine whether the similar fact evidence is collusion-free. If they decide that the evidence is not vitiated by collusion then they may rely upon it as evidence of the accused's guilt. If they are not satisfied that this is so, however, then they may not rely upon it for any purposes adverse to the defence.

At times it may appear to a judge in the course of a trial that no reasonable jury could decide that similar fact evidence was collusion-free. Where this is so, then the judge should direct the jury that they may not rely upon the evidence for purposes adverse to the defence.

Moreover, exceptionally, in determining the admissibility of similar fact evidence, a judge may find it necessary to take evidence of collusion into account when assessing the probative value of the similar fact evidence. This may be the case where, for example, evidence of collusion appears on the face of the documents before the judge. Consequently, there may be exceptional occasions upon which a judge will find it necessary to hold a *voir dire* in order to determine the admissibility of similar fact evidence.

Where the accused is being tried upon several similar counts and identification is in issue in relation to each, how should the jury be directed?

It may be that where an accused is tried upon two similar counts and identification is in issue in relation to each, the similarities between the two sets of facts are so striking that it is clear that the same person committed both offences. In such circumstances, there is authority to the effect that the trial judge should direct the jury that they cannot rely upon the similar fact evidence unless, independent of it, they are satisfied that the accused committed one of the offences (*R. v. McGranaghan* (1992)). Consideration of several more recent decisions of the Court of Appeal suggests, however, that the former approach is only required where identification is in issue and it is alleged that the fact that the accused committed one count proves that he also committed the other (see, for example, *R. v. Barnes* (1995)). In other circumstances, it appears to be proper to direct the jury that if they are satisfied that the same person committed both offences then they may consider the similar fact evidence in deciding whether the accused was the man (see, for example, *R. v. Downey* (1995) and *R. v. Barnes*).

When can objects discovered in the accused's possession provide evidence of his guilt?

Essentially, objects discovered in the accused's possession may be admissible as evidence of his guilt if relevant to an issue before the court but not merely for the purpose of proving that he has the disposition of one who commits offences of the type with which he is charged. Thus, for example, where equipment of a certain type was used in the commission of a crime, the fact that the accused had such equipment in his possession is clearly of relevance. In contrast, it appears that where such equipment was not used in committing the crime, the fact that the accused had such equipment in his possession will not be admissible for the purpose of identifying the accused as the offender even if persons who commit offences of the relevant type often use such equipment (see *R. v. Taylor* (1923)), unless there is other evidence identifying the accused as the offender and the evidence that the accused possessed the equipment is admitted in support of this other evidence (see *R. v. Reading* (1966)). Finally, it should be noted that even where evidence of the discovery of objects in the accused's possession is relevant to an issue before the court, the judge may refuse to admit such evidence upon the basis that the prejudicial effect of admitting it exceeds its probative value (*R. v. Reading* (1966)).

THE ADMISSIBILITY OF SIMILAR FACT EVIDENCE FOR THE DEFENCE IN CRIMINAL PROCEEDINGS

Similar fact evidence is only admissible for the defence in criminal proceedings if it is relevant to an issue before the court. Thus, one co-accused cannot make use of such evidence merely for the purpose of establishing that his co-accused has the disposition of one who commits offences of the type with which they are charged (*R. v. Neale* (1977)). In contrast, however, where such evidence either supports the accused's defence or damages the case against him, then it is admissible (see *R. v. Miller* (1952)). Further, it should be noted that where similar fact evidence is relevant, the judge cannot exclude it upon the basis that its probative value is outweighed by its prejudicial effect because he possesses no discretion to exclude defence evidence upon this basis (see *R. v. Miller*).

THE ADMISSIBILITY OF SIMILAR FACT EVIDENCE IN CIVIL PROCEEDINGS

Basically, similar fact evidence is admissible in civil proceedings if it is of relevance to an issue before the court and its admission is not "oppressive or unfair" to the other party (*Mood Music v. De Wolfe* (1976)). Such evidence is, however, not admissible in civil proceedings merely as evidence of a party's disposition (*Thorpe v. Chief Constable of Greater Manchester Police* (1989)). In the Mood Music case, a copyright action, the plaintiff was properly permitted to adduce evidence to the effect that the defendant had on several occasions produced musical works which were similar to those produced by others in order to rebut the defendant's assertion that the similarities between the two musical works which the case concerned was coincidental.

13. EVIDENCE OF CHARACTER

In this Chapter, we will consider: the nature of character evidence; the extent to which the accused in a criminal trial can adduce evidence of his good character and the relevance and effect of such evidence; the circumstances in which the accused may be cross-examined about his bad character and the purpose of such cross-examination.

WHAT IS MEANT BY "EVIDENCE OF CHARACTER"

The term "character", when considered in the context of the Law of Evidence, encompasses: evidence that a person is generally disposed to act in a particular way; evidence of specific instances in which a person acted in a particular way; and evidence as to a person's general reputation in his community. Evidence of character may be of good character (examples being that the witness has no previous convictions, is an upstanding member of the community, attends church regularly or contributes to several local charities) or of bad character (for example, he has several previous convictions or has been charged with a criminal offence).

The three most important issues to consider, and which will always feature in any answer to a problem type question on character, both good and bad, are admissibility, effect and relevance. The rules relating to the admissibility, effect and relevance of character evidence of the accused depend upon whether the accused chooses to testify or not, whether the evidence is of good or bad character and which party to the proceedings wishes to adduce the evidence.

EVIDENCE OF THE CHARACTER OF AN ACCUSED WHO CHOOSES NOT TO TESTIFY ON HIS OWN BEHALF

The admissibility, effect and relevance of evidence of the good or bad character of an accused who does not testify is governed by the common law.

Evidence of good character

Admissibility of evidence of good character A restrictive approach to the admissibility of evidence of the accused's good character was adopted in the leading case of *R. v. Rowton* (1865). The court held that only evidence of the accused's general reputation in the community would be admissible. Thus, an accused could not call witnesses to testify or, through his counsel, cross-examine prosecution witnesses, regarding specific examples of his good deeds or their favourable opinion of him. *Rowton* has never been overruled but has been applied flexibly by the courts. See, for example, *R. v. Redgrave* (1981) in which the accused was charged with importuning for immoral purposes. Although the accused was not permitted to adduce photographs of himself with women and love letters in support of his contention that he was heterosexual, the Court of Appeal stated that he might, at the court's discretion, have been allowed to adduce evidence to show that he had a normal sexual relationship with his female partner.

Relevance of evidence of good character At common law, admissible evidence of good character is relevant to the accused's guilt, *i.e.* to suggest to the court that, as a person of good character, he is unlikely to have committed the offence with which he is charged. Further, where the accused chooses not to testify but wishes to rely on exculpatory pre-trial answers or statements, he is also entitled to a direction on the relevance of his good character to the credibility of such statements (see *R. v. Vye* (1993)).

An accused who is of good character is entitled to a direction by the judge on the relevance of his good character even if he is jointly charged with an accused who is of bad character (see *R. v. Vye*).

The exclusionary discretion

The trial judge retains a discretion not to give the direction on the relevance of the accused's good character where he is satisfied that it would be an "insult to common sense" to do so, for example, where the accused has no previous convictions but it has been shown that he has engaged in serious criminal behaviour similar to the offence with which he is charged (see *R. v. Aziz* (1995)).

Effect of adducing evidence of good character An accused who raises his own good character is said to "put his character in issue". An accused who puts his character in issue and is of completely good character does not run any risk of harming his defence in so doing. However, if the accused who raises his good character is not, in fact, of completely good character, he runs the risk that the prosecution will adduce in rebuttal evidence relating to *any* aspect of his bad character, even evidence of character traits which were not raised by the defence. This is because a witness's character is treated as indivisible and it would mislead the court if only those aspects of the accused's character which were favourable to him were heard by the court (see *R. v. Winfield* (1939)).

If the accused does not call evidence of his own good character, but, instead, cross-examines prosecution witnesses as to their character, he puts their character in issue, not his own, and evidence of his bad character may not be adduced by the prosecution (see *R. v. Butterwasser* (1948)).

Relevance of evidence in rebuttal Where evidence of bad character is adduced in rebuttal, its relevance is unclear but, given that evidence of good character can be relevant to guilt, evidence in rebuttal is most likely to be also relevant to guilt.

Evidence of bad character

Admissibility, relevance and effect of evidence of bad character Subject to the common law exceptions listed below, evidence of the bad character of the accused is not admissible. The exceptions are: (*a*) where the evidence is admissible similar fact evidence—see Chapter 12 for consideration of the rules relating to the admissibility, effect and relevance of similar fact evidence, and (*b*) where the accused has put his character in issue—see above.

EVIDENCE OF THE CHARACTER OF AN ACCUSED WHO DOES TESTIFY ON HIS OWN BEHALF

The position of an accused who chooses to take the stand is governed by statute—section 1 of the Criminal Evidence Act 1898. Before considering in detail the admissibility, effect and relevance of character evidence under the statute, it is worth noting some points about section 1.

Points to note:

(1) *The "shield":* The relevant provisions of the Criminal Evidence Act 1898 are section 1(e) and, more importantly, section 1(f). Section 1(e) provides:

> "A person charged and being a witness in pursuance of this Act may be asked any question in cross-examination notwithstanding that it would tend to criminate him as to the offence charged."

Section 1(e) ought to be read along with section 1(f) which provides:

> "A person charged and called as a witness in pursuance of this Act shall not be asked, and if asked shall not be required to answer, any question tending to show that he had committed or been convicted of or been charged with any offence other than that wherewith he is then charged, or is of bad character, unless . . ."
>
> (i) the proof that he has committed or has been convicted of such other offences is admissible evidence to show that he is guilty of the offence wherewith he is then charged; or
>
> (ii) he has personally or by his advocate asked questions of the witnesses for the prosecution with a view to establish his own good character, or has given evidence of his good character, or the nature or conduct of the defence is such as to involve imputations on the character of the prosecutor or the witnesses for the prosecution, or the deceased victim of the alleged crime; or
>
> (iii) he has given evidence against any other person charged in the same proceedings."

It was recognised in *Jones v. DPP* (1962) that the combined effect of these two subsections is that the accused who testifies is given a "shield". This means that he cannot be cross-examined about his previous convictions, charges, etc., unless the shield is lost because one of the conditions specified in section 1(f)(i), (ii) or (iii) applies.

(2) Section 1(f) only prevents questioning of the accused "tending to show" he has previous convictions, etc. This term was

interpreted in *Jones* to mean "tending to show to the jury for the first time" or "tending to reveal". Thus, if the jury have already become aware of the accused's bad character, for example by the accused accidentally revealing it himself, the prosecution may cross-examine the accused about his convictions even though none of the conditions in section 1(f) apply.

(3) In addition to cross-examination about previous convictions and had character, an accused who has lost his shield may be cross-examined about any offence with which he has been "charged". In *Stirland* (1944), this term was interpreted as meaning **brought before a criminal court**. Two important issues which arise from this interpretation of the term are:

   (i) Is it permitted to cross-examine the accused about suspicions or accusations of criminal offences?
   (ii) Can an accused be cross-examined about his acquittals?
       Suspicions or accusations of criminal offences: In *Stirland*, the House of Lords held that questions regarding suspicions or accusations are inadmissible unless the accused has sworn expressly that he had never faced such accusations or suspicions.

Acquittals: The admissibility of questioning regarding acquittals was considered in *Maxwell v. DPP* (1935) where the court held that normally an accused ought not to be questioned about his acquittals as they are usually irrelevant in relation to his credit or guilt. The court did say, however, that exceptionally evidence of an acquittal could be relevant, and therefore admissible, an example being where statements made by the accused in the course of a previous trial in which the accused was acquitted may be admissible if their admission casts doubt upon evidence given by the accused in the instant proceedings.

(4) The shield may be lost under section 1(f)(i) if the accused's previous convictions are admissible as similar fact evidence. Subsection 1(f) is, however, largely irrelevant in practice. As Lord Morris pointed out in *Jones*, it is undesirable for similar fact evidence to be first raised in cross-examination, the reason being that the accused does not then have the opportunity of cross-examining prosecution witnesses about it.

(5) *The discretion:* Although the accused may lose his shield because one of the circumstances set out in section 1(f) apply, if the shield has been lost under section 1(f)(ii), he cannot be cross-examined by the prosecution about his previous convic-

tions, etc., without the leave of the court. The judge/magistrates retain a discretion to prevent such cross-examination. The circumstances in which it may be exercised are considered more fully later.

Evidence of good character

Admissibility of evidence of good character The extent to which an accused who testifies on his own behalf may adduce evidence of his good character, either by his own oral evidence or through examination of defence witnesses or through cross-examination of prosecution witnesses is, in theory, governed by the common law limitations set out in *Rowton*. Thus, the only evidence of good character which the accused would be able to adduce would be evidence of his general reputation in the community. However, in practice, an accused who has chosen to testify has sometimes been permitted to adduce evidence of good character outside the scope permitted by *Rowton*. In *Samuel* (1956), for example, the accused who was charged with larceny by finding, was allowed to adduce evidence of specific instances of his good character by asserting that he had, on two previous occasions, returned lost property to its owner.

Relevance of good character Evidence of the good character of the accused who chooses to testify is relevant to both credit (*i.e.* because he is of good character he is more likely to be speaking the truth than a person of bad character) and guilt (*i.e.* because he is of good character he is less likely to have committed the offence). This is so whether or not the accused is jointly charged with an accused of bad character (see *R. v. Vye*).

The discretion not to direct the jury on the relevance of the accused's good character, which was recognised in *R. v. Aziz*, above, applies equally to the accused who chooses to testify.

Effect of adducing evidence of good character An accused who testifies and puts his character in issue activates the first part of section 1(f)(ii) (see above). Thus, he will lose his shield and, subject to the court's discretion (which is rarely exercised when the shield is lost under the first part of section 1(f)(ii)), can be cross-examined by the prosecution about his previous convictions, charges, etc.

Examples of conduct which have activated this subsection, apart from the obvious example of an assertion of no previous convictions, include claims that the accused: is a family man in regular work (*R. v. Coulman* (1912); and is a religious man who has attended church services for a number of years (*R. v. Ferguson* (1909)).

Relevance of cross-examination under the first part of section 1(f)(ii) Where the first part of section 1(f)(ii) is activated, cross-examination is relevant to credit (see *R. v. Richardson & Longman* (1968)). It is unclear whether it is also relevant to guilt but there is dicta in *R. v. Samuel* (1956) to suggest that it might be so relevant.

Evidence of bad character

We have already seen above that the prosecution may cross-examine the accused about his bad character if he puts his character in issue. The other circumstances in which the shield may be lost under section 1(f), and the accused's bad character becomes admissible in cross-examination, are as follows.

Casting imputations—second part of section 1(f)(ii)

Admissibility of evidence of bad character Under the second part of section 1(f)(ii), the accused will lose his shield and may be cross-examined about his bad character if the nature or conduct of his defence is such as to involve imputations on the character of a prosecution witness or the deceased victim of the alleged offence.

Points to note:

(1) An imputation may be any allegation of discreditable conduct. It need not involve a criminal activity (see for example, *R. v. Bishop* (1975) in which an allegation that a witness was a homosexual amounted to an imputation).

(2) Imputations may be express or implied. An example of an express imputation is provided by *Lasseur* (1991) in which the accused alleged that a prosecution witness, who had been his former co-accused, was lying to achieve a lighter sentence. *R. v. Britzman* (1983) involved an implied imputation. The accused's allegation that, contrary to a police officer's evidence, a lengthy police interview had not taken place, was held to constitute an imputation because it amounted to an accusation that the police officer concerned had been lying to the court.

(3) In a rape case, the accused does not case an imputation on the complainant by alleging consent (see *Selvey v. DPP* (1970)).

(4) The imputation must be against the character of someone who is called to testify for the prosecution or against the dead victim of the accused. Thus, the accused may cast imputations with impunity upon anyone else (see *R. v. Westfall* (1912)).

(5) Once the judge determines that an imputation has been cast, the shield is lost even if it was necessary to the accused's defence that he make the imputation. See, for example, *R. v. Hudson* (1912) in which the accused lost his shield as a consequence of asserting that it was in fact a prosecution witness who had committed the offence with which he was charged. The fact that the accused had little choice as to whether to cast the imputation may, however, be taken into consideration by the trial judge in determining whether to exercise his discretion in the accused's favour (see *Selvey v. DPP* below).

The effect of casting imputations As soon as, in the opinion of prosecuting counsel, an imputation has been cast, he will ask the judge for leave to cross-examine the accused about his previous convictions. If the judge is satisfied that an imputation has been made, he will then consider whether to exercise his discretion to disallow cross-examination of the accused as to his bad character. If he decides not to exercise his discretion, the prosecution may then proceed to cross-examine the accused.

Relevance of cross-examination as a result of casting imputations Cross-examination under this part of section 1(f) is relevant only to the credit of the accused (see *R. v. McLeod* (1994)).

The discretion under section 1(f)(ii)

The judicial discretion in relation to cross-examination about the accused's bad character etc was recognised by the House of Lords in *Selvey v. DPP*. It applies to both parts of section 1(f)(ii) but is rarely exercised under the first part in favour of an accused who has attempted to mislead the court into believing he is of good character when he is not. As was explained in *R. v. Burke* (1985), the trial judge's discretion is completely unfettered and a higher court will not interfere with the exercise of that discretion unless the trial judge had erred in principle or there was no material on which he could properly have reached his decision. Thus, the trial judge may choose to disallow all questions relating to the accused's bad character, etc., only permit questions relating to certain offences and not others or permit questions about all the accused's previous convictions.

Which factors may be relevant to the exercise of the discretion? The following are merely guidelines set out in some of the leading cases which the trial judge may choose to take into consideration.

(i) Whether the imputation was a necessary part of the accused's defence (see *Selvey*).

(ii) The trial judge must ensure fairness to both sides by weighing the prejudicial effect of the questions to the defence against the damage done to the prosecution by the attack on their witness (see *Burke*).

(iii) If the credit of the prosecution witness has been attacked, it may be only fair that the court hear what kind of person the accused in fact is and whether he is any more worthy of belief than the prosecution witness (see *Burke*).

(iv) Because cross-examination under this subsection is relevant to credit only, one might expect the trial judge to exercise his discretion to prevent questions about offences not involving dishonesty which might be interpreted by the jury as being relevant to guilt. Such would be the case where the previous convictions are for offences which are similar to those charged but not sufficiently similar to be admissible as similar fact evidence. See, for example, *R. v. Watts* (1983) in which an accused charged with indecent assault was questioned about previous convictions for indecent assault on children. The Court of Appeal quashed the accused's conviction on the basis that the cross-examination was highly prejudicial (particularly since it involved offences against children) and had little probative value.

However, although *Watts* was probably correctly decided on its facts, the mere fact that the previous offences are of a similar nature and do not involve dishonesty will not necessarily lead to the exercise of the discretion in the accused's favour. In *R. v. Powell* (1985), the court stated that the fact that the previous convictions were of a similar nature and did not involve dishonesty were relevant considerations for the trial judge but they would not oblige him to exercise his discretion. The court emphasised that section 1(f)(ii) is a "tit for tat" section. Thus, if the accused attempts to discredit a prosecution witness, the prosecution ought to be allowed to discredit the accused by cross-examining him about *any* of his previous convictions, whatever their nature.

Giving evidence against a co-accused—section 1(f)(iii)

Admissibility of evidence of bad character An accused may lose his shield under section 1(f)(iii) and may be cross-examined about his had character if he has given evidence against any person charged in the same proceedings.

Must the defendants be charged with the same offence to activate section 1(f)(iii)? Provided the defendants are charged on the same indictment, it does not matter that they may be charged with different offences, section 1(f)(iii) can still be activated.

What is meant by "given evidence against"? This term was considered by the House of Lords in *Murdoch v. Taylor* (1965). The court held that hostile intent was not required in order to "give evidence against" because what was important was not the reason why one co-accused gave evidence against another but rather the effect of the evidence upon the minds of the jury. Thus, evidence which contradicts a co-accused's version of events will only amount to evidence against if it has the effect of supporting the prosecution's case against the co-accused in a material respect or undermining the defence of the co-accused.

Further guidance as to the term was provided in *R. v. Bruce* (1975) in which the Court of Appeal held that to activate section 1(f)(iii), evidence which undermines must reduce the accused's chances of acquittal. The facts of the case were that X and Y were jointly charged with robbery. X claimed that there had been a plan to commit the robbery but that he had played no part in the actual robbery. Y claimed tht he had not been involved and there had, in fact, been no plan to rob. The court held that Y's evidence had undermined X's defence but had not activated section 1(f)(iii) because it supplied X with a different defence and, therefore, did not make his acquittal less likely.

Will a denial by one co-accused of involvement in a joint venture amount to "giving evidence against"? A mere denial can have this effect but only in the situation in which, were the jury to accept the denial, it would work to the disadvantage of the co-accused. This can be illustrated by the facts of *R. v. Varley* (1982). A's version of events was that he had taken part in a robbery because he had been forced to do so by his co-accused, B. B denied being involved in the offence and alleged that A's version was false. The court held that B had given evidence against A because, were

B's version to be believed by the jury, it would have left A's defence
of duress high and dry and, therefore, undermined it.

The effect of giving evidence against Once the accused has
lost his shield under section 1(f)(iii), he may be cross-examined by
counsel for his co-accused. There is no discretion to disallow such
cross-examination (*Murdoch v. Taylor*) but the court does have a discretion to prevent cross-examination by the prosecution and,
indeed, will only allow such questioning in exceptional circumstances (see *R. v. Seighley* (1911)).

Relevance of cross-examination under section 1(f)(iii)
Cross-examination under this subsection is relevant to credit only
(see *Murdoch v. Taylor*).

---

14. SAMPLE QUESTIONS AND MODEL ANSWERS

QUESTION 1

Frank and his friend Michael have been jointly charged with
assaulting Diana. The prosecution allege that the defendants followed Diana home from a pub one night, grabbed her as she was
entering her house, dragged her inside and punched and kicked
her. Frank and Michael are both pleading not guilty.

Frank asserts that he and Michael had been drinking together
in the pub when Michael noticed Diana, with whom they had
attended the local school several years before. Michael had said
that he had always liked her but was too shy to ask her out and
asked Frank to go with him if he followed Diana home to find out
where she lived. Frank further asserts that he accompanied
Michael as they followed Diana home but left him at Diana's gate
and went home. Frank, who has two previous convictions for theft,
wishes to call Reverend Adams at trial to state that Frank is a lay
preacher at his church and regularly takes part in sponsored activities to raise funds for the new church roof.

Michael asserts that there was no plan to follow Diana and that
he left Frank at the pub and went straight home. Michael, who has
a previous conviction for kerb crawling and wasd once acquitted of
burglary, wishes to state at trial that Diana is blaming him and

Frank for the assault which had actually been inflicted by her boy-friend, Steve. He says she is blaming them because she is too afraid of Steve to blame him and has had a grudge against Frank and Michael since they testified against her brother resulting in his conviction for burglary last year.

Advise Frank and Michael of any evidential consequences of the way in which they intend to run their defences.

Answer

Frank and Michael both have previous convictions. In advising them, it is necessary to consider whether the way in which they intend to run their defences is such that the prosecution may be allowed to adduce evidence of their bad character, which would clearly damage their defences.

As Frank and Michael are non-compellable witnesses for the defence, they may each choose whether to testify on their own behalf. (However, should they decide not to testify, adverse infer-ences may be drawn from such failure under section 35 Criminal Justice and Public Order Act 1994). Whether the prosecution may adduce evidence of their bad character will depend upon whether or not they exercise this choice.

Should Frank and Michael elect not to testify, the extent to which evidence of their bad character may be adduced will be gov-erned by the common law. At common law, the prosecution may only adduce evidence of the accused's bad character if it is admiss-ible as similar fact evidence or the accused puts his character in issue by calling evidence as to his own good character. On the facts of this case, neither Frank's nor Michael's previous convictions would constitute admissible similar fact evidence. Michael does not intend to adduce evidence of his good character. Thus, if Michael does not testify on his own behalf, the prosecution will not be able to put his previous convictions before the court at his trial. How-ever, Michael may not have a very creditable defence if he does not testify—he is the only one who can refute Diana's assertion that he assaulted her and explain about her grudge against him and also refute Frank's assertion that he followed Diana home. Thus, Michael may decide to testify on his own behalf and run the risk that this may result in his previous convictions being put before the court.

Frank, on the other hand, does wish to call evidence of his good character. This raises three issues:

(i) can the Reverend Adams say what Frank wishes him to say;
(ii) if he can, what is the relevance of such evidence of good character;
(iii) what are the likely consequences of adducing such evidence.

With regard to the first issue, at common law the extent to which the accused may adduce evidence of his own good character is governed by the case of *Rowton*. In this case the court held that only evidence of the accused's general reputation in the community would be permitted, evidence of specific examples of good deeds or the witness's opinion of the accused would not. Applying the rule in *Rowton*, the Reverend Adams would be allowed to state that Frank is a lay preacher as this would be generally known. Strictly, applying *Rowton*, the Reverend Adams should not be permitted to state that Frank regularly raises funds for the new church roof as this is a specific example of Frank's good character. Since *Rowton* was decided, however, a slightly more flexible approach has been adopted by the courts, as illustrated in *Redgrave*, so it is possible that the trial judge might permit Reverend Adams to comment upon Frank's fund-raising activities, but this is uncertain.

Should the Reverend Adams be permitted to give evidence of Frank's good character, such evidence will be relevant to Frank's guilt, *i.e.* to show that, as a person of good character, he is unlikely to have committed the offence with which he is charged (*R. v. Vye*). Frank will be entitled to a direction from the judge to the jury to this effect even though he is jointly charged with Michael who is of bad character (*R. v. Vye*). The consequence of adducing evidence of his good character will be that he will have put his character in issue and the prosecution will be permitted to adduce evidence in rebuttal relating to any aspect of Frank's bad character, character being treated as indivisible (*Winfield*). Thus, the prosecution may adduce evidence of Frank's two previous convictions for theft. The relevance of these convictions is probably as to guilt although there is no clear authority on the point.

Should Frank and Michael decide to testify on their own behalf, their position will be governed by statute, the Criminal Evidence Act 1898. Section 1(f) of this statute provides the accused who testifies with a shield against cross-examination about his previous convictions. This shield may only be lost in the circumstances specified in section 1(f)(i)–(iii). It is, therefore, necessary to consider whether the way in which the accused intend to run their defence is likely to result in the loss of the shield and cross-examination about their previous bad character.

Frank

Frank wishes to adduce evidence of his good character. Since Frank is testifying, Reverend Adam's evidence will be relevant both to Frank's credit as a witness and to his guilt (*R. v. Vye*), *i.e.* that he is more likely to be speaking the truth and less likely to have committed the offence because he is of good character. Frank is entitled to a direction by the judge to this effect (*R. v. Vye*).

The effect on Frank's defence of putting his character in issue will be that he will lose his shield under section 1(f)(ii) and may be cross-examined by the prosecution as to his two previous convictions for theft. The judge retains a discretion under section 1(f)(ii) to prevent such cross-examination but it is rarely exercised in favour of an accused who puts his character in issue. The relevance of such cross-examination will be as to Frank's credit as a witness (*R. v. Richardson & Longman*). It is unclear whether it is also relevant to his guilt but there is dicta in *R. v. Samuel* to suggest that it is.

Frank also intends to state that he walked with Michael to Diana's gate and left him there. This clearly contradicts Michael's version of events and, should Frank say this at trial, he may activate section 1(f)(iii) and lose his shield. Section 1(f)(iii) provides that an accused will lose his shield if he has given evidence against any other person charged in the same proceedings. Frank and Michael are charged in the same proceedings and so, it is necessary to consider whether Frank's assertion will amount to giving evidence against Michael.

The term "given evidence against" was explained in *Murdoch v. Taylor*. The court stated that what was important was not the reason why an accused's testimony contradicted his fellow accused but the effect of his evidence on the minds of the jury. It would have to have the effect of supporting the prosecution's case against the accused in a material respect or undermining the defence of the co-accused. In order to determine whether this test is satisfied on the facts, it is necessary to consider what the effects would be on Michael's defence if Frank's assertion were believed by the jury. If the jury were to believe Frank, this would undermine Michael's defence because it puts him at the scene of the crime and he is asserting that he was never there. Thus, if Frank asserts that he left Michael at Diana's gate he will lose his shield under section 1(f)(iii) and may be cross-examined by Michael's counsel about his two convictions for theft. There is no discretion to prevent such cross-examination by counsel for a co-accused (*Murdoch v. Taylor*) although the court does have a discretion to prevent such cross-examination by the prosecution (*R. v. Seighley*). The relevance of cross-examination under section 1(f)(iii) is to credit only (*Murdoch v. Taylor*).

Michael

Michael also risks losing his shield under section 1(f)(iii). If his testimony is believed by the jury, it could be said to undermine Frank's defence, *i.e.* his assertion that he left the scene and Michael before any offence took place because Michael is stating that he was never there. If Michael is treated as giving evidence against Frank he, too, will lose his shield under section 1(f)(iii) and can be cross-examined by Frank's counsel as to his previous conviction for kerb crawling. Again, the relevance being as to his credit.

Whether he may also be cross-examined about his acquittal is more complex. An accused who loses his shield under section 1(f) may be cross-examined about any offence with which he has been "charged". This term was interpreted in *Stirland* to mean brought before a criminal court. Thus, in theory, an accused could be cross-examined about his acquittals. However, in *Maxwell v. DPP*, the court stated that normally an accused ought not to be cross-examined about an acquittal as it would be irrelevant. Exceptionally, evidence of an acquittal would be relevant and admissible if statements had been made in the earlier trial which cast doubt on the accused's evidence in the present proceedings. On the facts of this case, though, it is very unlikely that anything could have been said at the trial for burglary which would cast doubt upon what Michael is saying in his trial for assault. Thus, the acquittal would be deemed irrelevant and Michael could not be cross-examined about it.

Michael also intends to assert that it was actually Steve who assaulted Diana and it is only because she has a grudge against Michael and Frank that Diana is blaming them. These allegations against Steve and Diana will amount to imputations on their character, being allegations of discreditable conduct and, in the case of Diana, of actually lying, (in *R. v. Lasseur*, an allegation of lying was held to constitute an imputation). However, if Steve and Diana are not called as prosecution witness no harm will be done to Michael's defence by making these allegations (*R. v. Westfall*). Only if Steve or Diana or both testify for the prosecution will such allegations lead to loss of the shield under section 1(f)(ii). It is unclear whether Steve will be a prosecution witness but it is very likely that Diana, as the victim of the alleged assault, will be and so, Michael is likely to activate section 1(f)(ii). This is so even though he has to make the imputations as a necessary part of his defence (*Selvey v. DPP*).

Should Michael lose his shield under section 1(f)(ii), he may not be asked about his acquittal this, as we saw above, being irrelevant. Whether he may be cross-examined about his conviction for kerb crawling depends upon whether the trial judge exercises his discretion under section 1(f)(ii), recognised in *Selvey*, to disallow such questions.

There are several factors which the trial judge may take into account in deciding whether to exercise his discretion. First, whether the imputation was a necessary part of the accused's defence (*Selvey*)—it clearly was in Michael's case. Second, the trial judge must ensure fairness to both sides by weighing the prejudicial effect of the questions to the defence against the damage done to the prosecution by the attack on their witness (*R. v. Burke*). Third, the judge should bear in mind that section 1(f)(ii) is a "tit for tat" section and, if an attempt has been made to discredit a prosecution witness, the prosecution ought to be allowed to discredit the accused by cross-examining him about any of his previous convictions, whether or not they are for offences of dishonesty (*R. v. Powell*). Whatever decision the trial judge makes, it is very unlikely that a higher court will question his decision unless he has erred in principle or there was no material on which he could properly have reached his decision (*Burke*).

Should the trial judge permit cross-examination of Michael as to his conviction for kerb crawling, the cross-examination will be conducted by prosecution counsel and will be relevant to Michael's credit only (*McLeod*).

Finally, in advising both accused, I would advise them that if they wish to run their defences along the lines outlined in the question, it may be good tactics for them to both give evidence in chief as to their previous convictions. This would decrease the damage which would be done to their defence by being cross-examined about their convictions and may make the jury think more favourably of them for having volunteered evidence about their convictions without having been forced to do so.

QUESTION 2

Sylvia has been charged with criminal damage to her boyfriend's car. The prosecution allege that, upon finding out that Dave, her boyfriend, was also seeing his secretary behind her back, Sylvia went to Dave's office car park and poured paint stripper all over his brand new Mercedes, causing extensive damage. Sylvia denies damaging the car. The prosecution wish to rely upon the following items of evidence:

(1) Sylvia's admission when questioned by the police that she had damaged the car;
(2) the fact that, after her arrest, her house was searched and an empty can of paint stripper was found in her garage and when asked by the police officer to explain the can's presence in her garage she refused to say anything;
(3) the evidence of Bill, an elderly car park attendant, who saw a woman whom he described as being petite, in her late thirties and with long blond hair near the car (which was about 50 metres away) shortly before it was damaged. However, he was called away and did not see the actual damage occur. Bill later identified Sylvia at an identification parade as the woman he had seen near the car.

Sylvia is aged 23, has medium length mousy hair and is five feet nine inches tall. She says that she only admitted damaging the car because she is a diabetic and had been held at the police station for 24 hours without access to her insulin. She felt unwell and was anxious to get home for an injection of insulin but did not inform the police about her diabetes as she has always been acutely embarrassed about her illness and refuses to tell anyone about it. She had asked to see a solicitor but he was delayed and the police continued to question her in his absence. She confessed to the offence before her solicitor arrived.

Advise the prosecution as to:
 (i) the admissibility of Sylvia's admission;
 (ii) the evidential significance of Sylvia's refusal to explain the presence of the empty can of paint stripper in her garage;
 (iii) any evidential problems associated with the use of Bill's evidence.

Answer

Sylvia's admission

Sylvia's admission at the police station amounts to a confession, being adverse to her interests. As Sylvia admits making the confession but denies committing the offence, the issue of the admissibility of the confession will be heard on a *voir dire*. The confession will not be admissible unless the prosecution can prove beyond a reasonable doubt that the confession was not obtained as a result of oppression or in consequence of anything said or done which, in the circumstances existing at the time, was likely to render unreliable any confession which Sylvia might make in consequence thereof (section 76(2)(a) & (b) of PACE 1984). Thus, it is the manner in which the prosecution obtained the confession which is relevant, not the whether the confession may be true (*R. v. Crampton*).

As the prosecution must first prove that the confession was not obtained by oppression, it is necessary to define this term. Oppression has a partial definition in Sectiuon 76(8) as including ". . . torture, inhuman or degrading treatment, and the use or threat of violence (whether or not amounting to torture)." Clearly, Sylvia was not subjected to such treatment at the police station. However, as the statutory definition is not an all-encompassing definition, the courts have provided their own definition. In *Fulling*, the court gave the word its Oxford English Dictionary meaning which is, the "Exercise of authority in a burdensome, harsh or wrongful manner; unjust or cruel treatment of subjects, inferiors, etc.; the imposition of unreasonable or unjust burdens." Lord Lane C.J. took the view that improper conduct on the part of the interviewer was an essential ingredient of oppression as defined above. Sylvia has not had access to her insulin and was questioned in the absence of her solicitor. The failure to provide insulin would not constitute oppression as the police officers were not aware she was a diabetic and so there was no impropriety on their part in this regard. As for the questioning in the absence of her solicitor, the court stated, obiter, in *Alladice*, that refusal to allow acces to a solicitor, if accompanied by bad faith, might constitute oppression. Although a solicitor was in fact called in this case, Sylvia was questioned before he arrived which, unless properly authorised (of which there is no suggestion in the question), is contrary to section 58 of PACE. The court may treat this the same as if the police had refused to let Sylvia call a solicitor and, if the police acted in bad faith, this may amount to oppression. If it does, the confession will be excluded unless the prosecution can prove beyond a reasonable doubt that the confession was not obtained by the oppression, *i.e.* there was no casual link between the two.

Should the court determine that there was no oppression, or that if there was oppression that there was no casual link between the oppression and the confession, the prosecution must then prove that the confession was not obtained in consequence of anything said or done which (in the circumstances existing at the time) was likely to render any confession so obtained unreliable (section 76(2)(b). There is no statutory definition of unreliability but it is clear that impropriety is not required (*Fulling*). In approaching section 76(2)(b), the court must consider three issues:

  (i)   whether anything relevant was said or done;
 (ii)   the circumstances existing at the time;
(iii)   whether in those circumstances, the thing said or done was likely to render any confession unreliable.

On the facts, the something said or done could be the questioning in the absence of a solicitor (*Alladice*). The failure to provide insulin could not constitute something said or done as the interviewing officers were unaware of Sylvia's diabetes (*R. v. Goldenberg*). Her diabetes could, however, constitute a circumstance, despite the officers' ignorance of Sylvia's condition (*R. v. Everett*), as could her lack of legal advice. Should the court determine that something was said or done, the prosecution must prove beyond a reasonable doubt either that the accused did not confess in consequence of it or that it was not likely to render any confession unreliable. If they fail to do so, the confession will be excluded.

If the confession is not excluded under section 76, it may still be excluded by the judge in the exercise of his discretion, either at common law or under section 78 of PACE. Section 82(3) preserves the discretion which existed at common law but since the enactment of PACE, the courts have tended to rely on their exclusionary discretion under section 78. Section 78 permits the judge to exclude a confession if he considers that, having regard to all the circumstances, including the circumstances in which it was made, it would have such an adverse effect on the fairness of the proceedings that the judge ought not to admit it. In deciding whether to exercise his discretion, the judge may take into account the fact that there was a breach of PACE or the Codes of Practice. The police in this question appear to have breached section 58 of PACE. In *Walsh*, the court stated that if there was a significant or substantial breach of PACE or the Codes of Practice then prima facie the necessary standard of fairness has not been met but the breach must have such an adverse effect on the proceedings before the confession will be excluded. Breach of section 58 is likely to be treated as a significant and substantial breach, the right to access to a solicitor being described in *Samuel* as "fundamental". If the judge is satisfied that

Sylvia would probably not have confessed had questioning been delayed until her solicitor arrived, he is likely to exercise his discretion to exclude (*Samuel*). If the judge is not satisfied of this, he may still exclude if the police officers' decision to continue questioning amounted to a deliberate decision not to comply with the requirements of PACE (*Alladice*).

Sylvia's refusal to explain the presence of the empty can of paint stripper

Under section 36 of the Criminal Justice and Public Order Act 1994, the court may draw such inferences as appear proper from the fact that an arrested person, when asked to account for the presence in his possession of an object which the investigating officer believes may have been used in the commission of an offence, failed to so account. Sylvia had been arrested before being asked to explain the presence of the paint stripper can (which the police officer would obviously consider had been used in the offence) in her possession. Thus, subject to the trial judges exclusionary discretion under section 36(6) of the Act, the court will be able to draw an inference from her failure to provide an explanation. Although Sylvia cannot be convicted solely upon such an inference, it may contribute to a prima facie case against her (section 38(3)).

Bill's identification of Sylvia

Bill has positively identified Sylvia at an ID parade, an ID which Sylvia disputes. Thus, the *Turnbull* ID guidelines will apply. The judge must warn the jury of the special need for caution when deciding whether to place reliance upon the evidence of an identification witness and explain to them that an ID witness may, though very convincing, still be mistaken. The judge should direct the jury to consider the circumstances in which the witness observed the accused, pointing out any weaknesses and discrepancies between the description given by the witness and the actual appearance of the accused. On the facts of this case, the judge should point out to the jury the discrepancies in terms of Sylvia's age, height and length and colour of hair and also direct them to consider whether Bill's eyesight may not be particularly good given his age and whether, at a distance of 50m, he could have clearly seen the person standing next to the car. The ID evidence in this case appears poor and, if there was no other evidence to support the identification, the judge would be obliged, under the guidelines, to withdraw the case from the jury and direct an acquittal. However, the ID is supported by Sylvia's refusal to account for the can of paint stripper and, if admissible, her confession. Thus, it is unlikely that the judge would withdraw the case from the jury.

QUESTION 3

Henry has been charged with the murder of Mandy and is pleading not guilty. The prosecution allege that Henry shot his estranged wife as she walked home from her night class. Shortly after the shooting, Mandy was found by a passer by, Tom. Before she lapsed into unconsciousness, she said to Tom, "I don't know if I'll survive this but if I don't, I want you to make sure that Henry pays for what he has done to me." Mandy regained consciousness in hospital two days later and made a statement to a police officer, PC Plodd, naming Henry as her assailant. PC Plodd wrote her statement down in his notebook. However, Mandy lapsed into unconsciousness again before PC Plodd could read her statement back to her to check its accuracy. Mandy died shortly after.

Advise the prosecution as to the admissibility of Mandy's statements to Tom and PC Plodd.

Answer

Mandy's statement to Tom

Mandy's statement to Tom was an out of court statement (it was made at the scene of the stabbing) which the prosecution would be seeking to adduce to prove the truth of its factual content (the implied meaning of what Mandy was saying was that it was Henry who shot her). For this reason, Mandy's statement would be implied as hearsay, the hearsay rule applying to implied hearsay in the same way as it applies to express hearsay (*Kearley*). Thus, her statement would be prima facie inadmissible so Tom could not repeat it in court. Tom could only repeat Mandy's statement if an exception to the hearsay rule applied, *e.g.* dying declaration or res gestae.

The dying declaration exception permits a witness to give hearsay evidence concerning the cause and circumstances of a victim's death as an exception to the hearsay rule in murder cases provided the original maker of the statement made the statement whilst under a settled hopeless expectation of death (*Perry*). A settled hopeless expectation of death means tht the maker of the statement must have abandoned all hope of living (*Hayward*). Clearly, Mandy had not abandoned all hope of living when she made her statement to Tom as she said, "I don't know if I'll survive ...". Thus, Tom could not repeat Mandy's statement under this exception.

The *res gestae* exception permits a witness to give hearsay evidence of a statement provided that at the time when the statement was made the mind of its maker was so dominated by a dramatic event that the possibility of concoction can be excluded (*Andrews*). Only if the statement was made in circumstances of contemporaneity with the dramatic event can the possibility of concoction be disregarded, though precise contemporaneity is not required provided that, on the facts, the possibility of concoction can properly be excluded. The trial judge should pay particular attention to any factors which might increase the risk of concoction (such as whether the maker had a grudge against the accused) and to any special factors which might give rise to the possibility of error (*e.g.* whether the maker was intoxicated at the time when he made the statement). Mandy's statement was made shortly after the stabbing. Tom may repeat it in court provided that the judge (taking into account any factors which may give rise to an increased risk of fabrication and of any special factors giving rise to a risk of error) is satisfied that Mandy's mind was dominated by the shooting at the time when she made it.

The statement to PC Plodd

(a) *The oral testimony of PC Plodd:* Mandy's statement to PC Plodd is also hearsay as it was made out of court (at the hospital) and would be adduced by the prosecution to prove the truth of its factual content (that Henry shot Mandy). Thus, PC Plodd could not repeat Mandy's statement in court unless an exception to the hearsay rule were to apply to the statement.

The question does not make clear whether, when Mandy made the statement, she was under a "settled hopeless expectation of death". The dying declaration exception will only apply if this was the case. It is unlikely that the *res gestae* exception would apply because it is difficult to argue that Mandy's mind would be so dominated by the exciting event after a two-day time gap so as to exclude the possibility of concoction. [One might argue, however, that since Mandy had been in a coma for most of the time between making her two statements she had had no opportunity for concoction prior to making the second, though there is no authority to suggest that the court would accept such an argument.] If it is admissible, PC Plodd may repeat Mandy's statement in court. If he has difficulty in remembering exactly what Mandy said, he can refresh his memory in the witness box by referring to his notebook because a witness may refresh his memory from a document made at the same time as the events the document describes (*Richards*) and PC Plodd wrote down Mandy's statement as she made it.

(b) *PC Plodd's notebook:* If the judge determines that PC Plodd may not repeat Mandy's statement, his notebook may still be admissible as an exception to the hearsay rule under section 23 or section 24 of the Criminal Justice Act 1988. Section 23 permits a documentary hearsay statement to be admitted provided the statement was made in the document and there is a statutory reason for not calling the maker of the statement. Although there is a statutory reason for not calling the maker, *i.e.* that she is dead, Mandy did not make her statement in the notebook as she did not acknowledge its accuracy (*McGillivray*). Thus, the statement in the notebook will not be admissible under section 23.

The statement may be admitted under section 24 as it is located in a document, the document was received in the course of a profession (by PC Plodd in his capacity as the officer investigating the offence) and the supplier of the information (Mandy) had personal knowledge of the events she described in her statement. However, because the statement was prepared for the purposes of a criminal investigation, one of the reasons specified in section 23 or section 24(4)(b)(iii) for not calling the maker of the statement must be established. In *Brown v. Secretary of State for Social Security*, the court held that the maker of a statement for the purposes of section 24 is the person who took down what the supplier told him. Thus, applying *Brown*, the maker in this case is PC Plodd and there is no statutory reason for not calling him. Upon this basis, the statement would be inadmissible under section 24. If one argues, however, that *Brown* was incorrectly decided because it requires a reason for not calling someone whose oral evidence would have been inadmissible as hearsay anyway and, indeed, it was not followed in *R. v. Lockley*, then the maker of the statement would be the actual supplier of the information who, upon the facts of this question, would be Mandy. There is a statutory reason for not calling Mandy in that she is dead and consequently, if *Brown* is incorrect, the statement would be admissible under section 24.

If the statement is admissible under section 24, the prosecution

will have to obtain the leave of the court to admit it as it was
obtained for the purposes of a criminal investigation (section 26).
The judge will only grant leave if he considers it in the interests of
justice to do so. The judge also retains a discretion to exclude evidence otherwise admissible under section 23 or section 24 if he considers it in the interests of justice to do so (section 25). If the judge
decided to grant leave to admit the statement, it is unlikely that
he would proceed to exclude it in the exercise of his discretion
(*Grafton*).

QUESTION 4

Fred is charged with raping his two daughters, Barbara, aged 17,
and Julie, aged 13. Barbara alleges that, from the age of 10 until
she left home, aged 15, Fred regularly had sexual intercourse with
her without her consent. Julie alleges that from the time when
Barbara left home until the time when she (Julie) was taken into
care, Fred regularly had sexual intercourse with her without her
consent. Both daughters claim that neither they nor their mother,
Audrey, dared to inform the police of their father's conduct because
he had threatened to kill them all if they did so. Fred denies the
charges and claims that Audrey, Barbara and Julie fabricated the
entire story in order to punish him when he left Audrey for another
woman.

The counts relating to Barbara and Julie are being jointly tried
in Oxgate Crown Court. Consider whether:

(a) Julie is likely to be a competent prosecution witness;
(b) Audrey can be compelled to testify for the prosecution;
(c) the jury are likely to be permitted to consider the evidence
    relating to the alleged rape of Barbara upon the trial of the
    count relating to Julie and whether they are likely to be
    permitted to consider the evidence relating to the alleged
    rape of Julie upon the trial of the count relating to Barbara;
(d) the trial judge is required to warn the jury of the danger of
    relying upon the evidence of any or all of Audrey, Barbara
    and Julie.

Answer

(a) A witness is competent if the court may receive the witness's
testimony. A witness is compellable if the witness may be required
to testify. Julie is under fourteen years of age and, consequently, is

a child for the purposes of section 33A of the Criminal Justice Act 1988. Thus, Julie cannot give sworn evidence but may give unsworn evidence unless, in the opinion of the judge, she is incapable of giving intelligible testimony. She will be capable of giving intelligible testimony if she can understand questions and give coherent and comprehensive answers (*DPP v. M*). The judge may examine her before she testifies in order to determine her competence or may decide to permit her to testify, subject to the possibility of standing her down and striking her testimony out if it should prove to be unintelligible (*R. v. Hampshire*). If the judge examines her before she testifies he may do so in the absence of the jury (*Hampshire*).

[***Note***: If Julie is competent the court may permit her to testify by live television link (Criminal Justice Act 1988, s.32) or may permit her to give evidence by video recorded interview (Criminal Justice Act 1988, s.32A) (see Chapter 4 above).]

(b) In general, the spouse of the accused is a competent prosecution witness but cannot be compelled to testify (Police and Criminal Evidence Act 1984, s.80).

The spouse is not a competent prosecution witness if the spouse and the accused are jointly charged with an offence. The spouse is a compellable prosecution witness if the offence with which the accused is charged falls within section 80(3) of the Police and Criminal Evidence Act 1984. The offences with which Fred is charged do fall within that section (they are sexual offences allegedly committed in respect of persons who were under 16 years of age at the material time).

Thus, Audrey appears to be a competent and compellable prosecution witness.

(c) The question is whether the evidence of each daughter is likely to be admissible as similar fact evidence in relation to the trial of the count relating to the other. In order to be admissible, such evidence must be relevant to an issue before the court and must not merely be adduced in order to establish the accused's disposition to commit offences to the relevant type (*Makin v. Attorney-General for New South Wales*). Further, such evidence is only admissible if, in the opinion of the trial judge, the prejudicial effect which results from its admission is outweighed by its probative value (*Boardman v. DPP*).

Here, the evidence of each daughter appears to be relevant not merely to establish their father's disposition but, rather, as in *DPP v. P*, to confirm the other's evidence. The evidence is clearly extremely prejudicial, and it is for the trial judge to decide whether this prejudice is outweighed by its probative value.

If the identity of the rapist was in dispute, then striking similarity would normally be required in order to provide sufficient probative value to justify the admission of the similar fact evidence (*DPP v. P*). This is not the case, however, and so, even though there is no striking similarity on these facts (*i.e.* no repetition of unusual features), the judge may still be able to identify a sufficient degree of probative value to justify the admission of the evidence.

If evidence suggesting that Audrey, Barbara and Julie have fabricated their evidence appears on the documents, the judge may decide to take this into account in determining whether the similar fact evidence is admissible (*R. v. H*). If this is the case, the judge may, exceptionally, find it necessary to hold a voir dire before deciding whether to admit the similar fact evidence. Normally, however, the judge should not take an assertion of collusion into account in determining whether similar fact evidence is admissible (*R. v. H*).

Rather, it is normally for the jury to determine whether similar fact evidence is collusion-free. If the jury decides that it is, then the jury may rely upon it. If the jury is not satisfied that the similar fact evidence is collusion-free, however, then the jury may not rely upon it as evidence against the accused (*R. v. H*).

Finally, if, in the course of the trial, the judge decides that no reasonable jury could find that the similar fact evidence was collusion free, then he should direct the jury not to rely upon it as evidence against Fred (*R. v. H*).

[**Note**: on facts such as the present, if in the opinion of the judge the probative value of the similar fact evidence does not outweigh its prejudicial effect, an application by the accused to have the two counts tried separately would be likely to succeed (see *DPP v. P*).]

(d) A trial judge is no longer required to give the jury a corroboration warning in respect of the evidence of children (Criminal Justice Act 1988, s.34(2)), accomplices or sexual offence complainants (Criminal Justice and Public Order Act 1994, s.32(1)). The role of the trial judge following this statutory reform was considered by the Court of Appeal in *R. v. Makanjuola*.

Essentially, it appears that whilst the judge may give a warning he is not required to do so merely because Barbara and Julie are sexual offence complainants or because Julie is a child. Rather, a warning should only be given if there is an evidential basis for suggesting that a witness is unreliable.

In this case, the fact that Jack left Audrey for another woman may provide an evidential basis for the suggestion that Audrey and her two daughters have a grudge against Fred. Consequently, the judge may feel that it is necessary to warn the jury to be cautious when relying on the evidence or Barbara or on that of either daughter. If he is particularly concerned that the evidence may be unreliable, the judge may go further and advise the jury to look for evidence supporting the potentially unreliable evidence before relying on it.

[**Note**: if the jury is not satisfied that the evidence is collusion-free then the jury should not consider the evidence of each daughter in relation to the trial of the count concerning the other (see part (c) of this question, above).]

QUESTION 5

Jack, a travelling salesman, is bringing an action in negligence against Amanda in Oxgate County Court in respect of an accident in which his car was damaged when he swerved and left the road in order to avoid a car driven by Amanda which was heading towards him on the wrong side of the road. Immediately after Jack swerved, Amanda collided with a car driven by Tom, both her car and the car driven by Tom being damaged in the collision.

Following the accident, Amanda was convicted of dangerous driving by Oxgate Crown Court. Tom then successfully brought an action in negligence against her, recovering damages in respect of the damage to his car.

Amanda claims that Jack's accident was not her fault because, immediately prior to it, the steering of her car had failed and this had caused her car to veer onto the other carriageway. Further, Amanda has obtained possession of a letter concerning the accident, written by Jack to his solicitor, Eric, in which Jack stated,

"I had been driving for four hours when the accident took place. If I hadn't been half asleep and had been concentrating I'm sure that I could have avoided her car without crashing."

The letter was stolen from a file in Eric's office by a friend of Amanda's who works for Eric.
Consider whether:

(a) Jack may successfully assert that Amanda is estopped from denying Jack's allegation of negligence in consequence of

      the successful action in negligence which Tom brought
      against her;

(b) Amanda's conviction will be admissible in evidence for Jack;

(c) if Amanda asserts that Jack and she were equally to blame
for the accident, she will bear the burden of proving this
and, if so, to what standard;

(d) Amanda can call Mr Smith, the mechanic who maintains
her car, to state in court that he examined the car after the
accident and that, in his opinion, the steering had probably
failed before she crashed into Tom.

(e) Jack can prevent Amanda from adducing in evidence the
letter which he wrote to his solicitor.

Answer

(a) Neither a cause of action estoppel nor an issue estoppel can lie
in these circumstances for two reasons.

First, in order for an estoppel to lie, the parties to the latter
proceedings must be the parties to the former proceedings or their
privies. Here, however (as in *Townsend v. Bishop*), the parties are
different (Tom and Amanda being the parties to the first proceedings and Jack and Amanda being the parties to the second).

Secondly, in order for an estoppel to lie the cause of action or
issue which is being litigated in, the latter proceedings must have
been determined in the former proceedings (see, for example,
Brunsden v. Humphrey). Here, however, neither the cause of action
nor any issue which Jack and Amanda are litigating were determined in the proceedings between Tom and Amanda (the first proceedings determining that Amanda was to blame for the collision
in which Tom's car was damaged, the second concerning her liability with regard to the damage to Jack's car when it left the road).

(b) Amanda's conviction for dangerous driving is clearly of relevance in determining whether she was negligent in the context of
the action brought by Jack. Consequently, the conviction will be
admissible under section 11 of the Civil Evidence Act 1968. Under
section 11, Amanda will be taken to have committed the offence
unless the contrary is proved. It is unclear, however, whether, if
Amanda asserts that she did not commit the offence, the conviction
amounts to evidence to the effect that she did (*Stupple v. Royal
Insurance Co Ltd*). It appears, however, that proving that she did not
commit the offence will be a difficult task (*Hunter v. Chief Constable
of the West Midlands Police*).

(c) The party who raises an issue is required to prove it (see, for example, *Wakelin v. London and South Western Railway*). Jack, the plaintiff, bears the burden of proving those issues which he has raised (essentially, that Amanda owed him a duty of care, that her conduct amounted to a breach of that duty and that, in consequence of her breach of duty, he suffered loss). Amanda, the defendant, bears the burden of proving those issues which she raises (though she bears no burden of proof merely because she denies assertions made by Jack). Thus, since Amanda raises the issue of whether Jack is partly to blame for the damage which he suffered, the burden of proof in relation to the defence of contributory negligence lies on her.

The requisite standard of proof in civil proceedings is proof on a balance of probabilities. Thus, in order to establish her defence, Amanda must essentially persuade the judge that it is more probable than not that Jack's negligence was a contributory cause of his accident (*Miller v. Minister of Pensions*).

(d) Expert opinion evidence is only admissible in relation to an issue where the court requires the assistance of an expert in order to determine that issue (see, for example, *R. v. Smith*). It would appear that a judge would require the opinion of an expert witness in order to determine whether Amanda's steering had failed prior to her collision with Tom. Thus, it appears that expert evidence is admissible in this context.

Further, a witness is only competent to give expert evidence if he is an expert. Formal training and/or qualifications are not required provided that the witness has obtained the necessary expertise (see, for example, *R. v. Stockwell*). If the judge is satisfied that Mr Smith is qualified to give expert evidence on this issue then he may receive his evidence.

Finally, unless Jack agrees to the admission of the expert evidence or Amanda obtains the leave of the court, she must apply to the court for a direction on disclosure with which she must comply (CCR, Ord. 20). The court will probably require Amanda to disclose Mr Smith's evidence to Jack in the form of a written report. The court may also direct that Mr Smith meet Jack's expert witness (if he has one) in order to determine whether any parts of their evidence are in dispute. Further, either Amanda or Jack may put the written report in evidence.

[**Note**: it appears that, in April 1999, the Supreme Court and County Court Rules will be replaced by the Civil Procedure Rules, which may significantly modify this part of the answer to question five. Unfortunately, the new rules are not available at the time of writing.]

(e) The statement contained in the letter written by Jack to his solicitor is a hearsay statement because it was not made in court in the course of the proceedings between Jack and Amanda and is being used in court to prove the truth of its factual content (merely that Jack was partly to blame for the damage which he suffered) (see, for example, *Myers v. DPP*). Whilst the statement is an informal admission, such statements no longer fall within a pre-served common law exception to the hearsay rule (Civil Evidence Act 1995, s.7). The statement will, however, fall within the general exception to the hearsay rule contained in section 1 of the 1995 Act. Amanda should serve a hearsay notice on Jack in accordance with section 2 of the 1995 Act and with rules of court (failure to serve such a notice will not affect the admissibility of the evidence but may result in an adjournment and/or have cost implications). Amanda may make use either of the original letter or of a copy (authenticated in a manner approved by the court) in order to prove the statement (section 8). In the circumstances (see section 4), the evidential weight of the statement will probably be high (it is unlikely that the plaintiff would flippantly make such a state-ment adverse to his interests).

Section 1 of the 1995 Act does not make a hearsay statement admissible if it was excluded by some rule of evidence other than the rule against hearsay (*e.g.* the opinion evidence rule). Whilst Jack's statement is opinion evidence, section 3(2) of the Civil Evid-ence Act 1972 makes non-expert opinion evidence admissible, even in relation to an ultimate issue, to prove facts which a witness per-sonally perceived.

A communication in confidence between a client and his legal adviser for the purpose of obtaining or giving legal advise is subject to legal professional privilege (see, for example, *Balabel v. Air India*). Thus, upon the assumption that Jack wrote the letter for the pur-pose of obtaining legal advice, had the letter not fallen into Amanda's possession, Jack could refuse to produce it or to answer questions concerning its contents and could require his solicitor to do the same. Since the letter has fallen into Amanda's hands, how-ever, she will be able to adduce it in evidence unless Jack obtains an injunction ordering her to return the letter to him. Further, if she has made copies of the letter, he will require the injunction to prevent her from using the copies as secondary evidence of the letter's contents in the course of the proceedings between Jack and herself (see *Calcraft v. Guest* and *Lord Ashburton v. Pape*). If the letter has already been adduced in evidence then he will be too late to obtain an injunction (*Goddard v. Nationwide Building Society*). Moreover, the court may refuse to grant him an injunction in the exercise of its equitable discretion (*e.g.* if there has been undue delay in applying for it) (*Goddard v. Nationwide Building Society*).

INDEX